WHAT A YEAR IT WAS!

1956

A walk back in time to revisit
what life was like in the year that
has special meaning for you...

*Congratulations
and
Best Wishes*

To

From

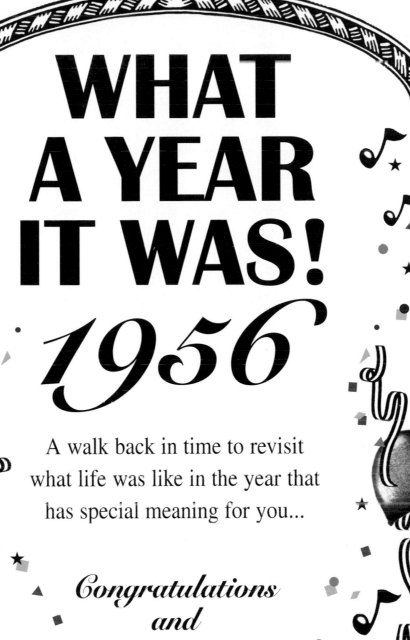

DEDICATION

To My Children—Lee, Laurie, Melanie And Sweet Danielle
Thank You For Your Love, Support And Sense Of Humor

Designer • Peter Hess
Production Supervisor • Carol Davis
Researcher • Laurie Cohn

CONTENTS

POLITICS AND 1956

WORLD EVENTS

Military observers from Western Allied Headquarters arrive in Brandenburg to witness a token withdrawal of Red forces from East Germany as part of Russia's withdrawal proposal.

RED TROOPS WITHDRAW— CUT DOWN NUMBER OF TROOPS IN EAST GERMANY

WHAT A YEAR IT WAS!

5

1956

Involved in the operation is the removal of 89 obsolescent planes and the first contingent of 50,000 troops that Russia announced it will demobilize.

A Russian photographer records the evacuation which is part of an overall reduction of Russian troops.

NAVY BASE REGAINED BY FINLAND

CIRCULATION 3

DAILY

With the signing of the treaty relinquishing the Russian naval base on Finnish soil, Finnish soldiers arrive to take over the 220-square mile base.

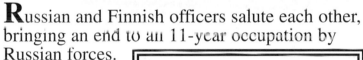

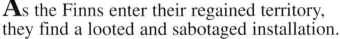

Russian and Finnish officers salute each other, bringing an end to an 11-year occupation by Russian forces.

Photographers capture this historic moment.

As the Finns enter their regained territory, they find a looted and sabotaged installation. Power houses are dismantled and gun emplacements are destroyed.

Every trace of Russian occupation is destroyed and all Scandinavia breathes easier as Red guns cease to dominate the Baltic.

Beautiful new way to bring back the colorful moments of your life..... life-size

Files and safeguards slides! Aluminum magazines keep precious slides in perfect, indexed order. Individual metal frames protect them from dirt, smudges, dog-earing. Your fingers never touch the transparencies.

Spectacular picture quality! A powerful, 4-inch wide-angle lens gives you big-as-life pictures that let the whole family enjoy the show even in a small room.

NEW ARGUS AUTOMATIC PROJECTOR $59⁵⁰
complete with carrying case, automatic slide changer, slide editor and 36-slide magazine

You've photographed the big moments of your life in color. Now relive them—big as life and just as colorful—with this new Argus Automatic!

A new, advanced optical system delivers more light through the wide-angle lens to give you pictures uniformly bright and clear, from corner to corner.

And your slides are so easy to show. A quick push-pull of the operating handle positions each slide for perfect viewing, returns it to the magazine in order, and automatically advances the next slide.

A convenient Slide Editor lets you pre-view slides before you file them in the magazine. And a powerful yet silent blower keeps projector and slides cool—even during long showings.

To see your color slides in a beautiful new light, see the all-new Argus line of 300-Watt Projectors at your dealer's now.

Standard model, with non-automatic operation, $37.50. New Remote-Control Power Unit for any Argus Automatic, runs the show by push-button from anywhere in the room, $24.50.

argus ®

Easy to use...Easy to own...That's Argus!
Most dealers offer convenient credit terms

8

BRITAIN AND U.S. ISSUE JOINT STATEMENT

President Eisenhower and Britain's Prime Minister, Sir Anthony Eden, conclude three days of talks in Washington on world problems with the issuance of a joint warning to the people of Asia and Africa on the dangers of economic and political help from the Soviet Union.

The two world powers further pledge joint action to defend the peace in the Middle East.

WHAT A YEAR IT WAS!

9

ARGENTINEANS RALLY

Several hundred thousand people mass in the Plaza Congreso to demonstrate their faith in the current regime with cries of "Libertad."

After a decade of rule by dictator Juan Peron, the crowd jeers his name as speaker after speaker condemns his iron rule of the Republic.

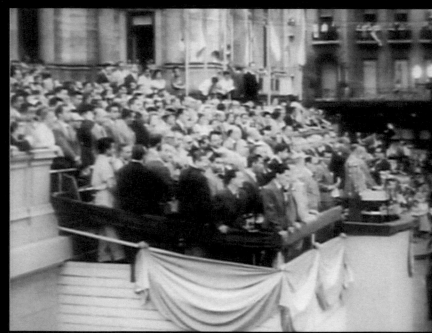

The U.S.S. Boston, America's first guided missile cruiser, pictured in maneuvers off Cuba. Ship and missile are designed for each other in what engineers call an integrated weapons system.

From below deck magazines, the missiles, with lethal capabilities, are positioned on launching racks where a full salvo can be aimed and fired in seconds and guided to the target while in flight.

THE NAVY OF TOMORROW

With the U.S.S. Boston, the guided missile comes into its own.

AMERICA TAKES REVOLUTIONARY STEP FORWARD IN NAVAL WARFARE AND THE NATION'S DEFENSE

The atomic submarine Nautilus passes all tests with flying colors, cruising submerged a distance equivalent to circling the globe.

Guided missiles with increased range are added to the undersea arsenal and the submarine becomes a more formidable weapon of counterattack on enemy coasts.

The Symbol that links the bounty of the sea to your pantry shelves

Fish from the waters of Maine and California . . . from far-away Alaska and the Gulf of Mexico . . . come to your pantry today with extra flavor and nutrition because of the can and a symbol you probably seldom notice.

The symbol is a trade-mark—a small oval on the ends of cans made by American Can Company.

Back of it is Canco's belief that the can is more than a container; it's a way of helping you live better . . . more conveniently . . . for less money.

Back of it, too, is Canco's motto "Can do," and the *spirit of cooperation* that makes this motto work.

BEHIND THIS SYMBOL ARE THE SERVICES OF CANCO'S "CAN DO" MEN. HERE'S HOW THEY HELP BRING YOU TASTIER CANNED FISH.

AS ANY FISHERMAN KNOWS, the quicker fish is prepared after catching, the better the flavor. To help the industry preserve flavor and cut catch-to-can time, Canco was first to develop high-speed machinery to fill cans and close under vacuum.

FOOD CHEMIST L. G. GERMAIN is one of the many specialists who help the fishing industry produce better products. Faced with tough problems and great opportunities, Canco's researchers and service people have always answered "Can do"!

 "Can do"... *that's the spirit of* American Can Company

13

1956

TURBULENT ELECTION IN KOREA

The most turbulent election in Korea's young history as a republic swings into high gear with public interest at a high pitch.

President Rhee *(right)* faces strong opposition for the first time from Democratic party leader, P.H. Shinicky.

Shinicky makes his first campaign speech to an enthusiastic crowd. Later, he suffers a fatal heart attack leaving Rhee virtually unopposed.

With the sudden death of Shinicky, tension mounts as his followers take to the streets, some of whom storm President Rhee's palace.

WHAT A YEAR IT WAS!

Marshal Tito of Yugoslavia arrives in Paris for a state visit.

Accompanied by his wife, Tito is welcomed by a corps of French government officials.

Extreme security measures are taken as France has not forgotten the assassination of King Alexander of Yugoslavia 22 years ago.

Guards are alerted as Tito arrives at the Palais de L' Elysée.

President Coty decorates Marshal Tito with the Military Cross for actions against Hitler.

WHAT A YEAR IT WAS!

15

SALUTE TO IKE—PRESIDENT ADDRESSES DINERS IN 53 CITIES

MADISON SQ. GARDEN

TONITE N Y & N J
SALUTE TO IKE
HOLLYWOOD ICE REVUE
NIGHTLY THRU JAN 30
MAT SAT & SUN

Madison Square Garden in New York sets the pace in the national Salute To Ike dinners across the nation.

10,000 Republicans gather and eat $100 box dinners to help swell campaign coffers for the coming election.

The President and Mrs. Eisenhower acknowledge the applause of his supporters.

➤ President Eisenhower Names Citizens' Board To Monitor The Activities Of The CIA As Well As Other Security Gathering Agencies.

➤ George Meany Recommends To Democratic Platform Committee Federal Minimum Hourly Wage Be Raised To $1.25 And Tax Cuts For The Lower-Income Bracket.

➤ Senator John F. Kennedy Edged Out Of Presidential Ticket As Democrats Name Senator Estes Kefauver As Adlai E. Stevenson's Running Mate.

➤ Senator John F. Kennedy Appeals To Democrats To End Party Dissension That Could Lead To More Victories For The Republicans.

➤ Women In Congress Reaches Sixteen — A Record High.

➤ President Eisenhower Authorizes Sale Of Uranium For Production Of Atomic Power Domestically And Abroad For Non-Military Use.

➤ Test Pilot Killed As World's Fastest And Highest Altitude Airplane—U.S. Air Force's Bell X-2—Crashes.

➤ Russia Leads In H-Bomb Planes.

➤ Soviet Complaints Lead To U.S. Halting The Launching Of Weather Balloons.

➤ U.S. Air Force Radar Detection Platform Designed To Scan The Atlantic Ocean For Aircraft Is Installed Off Of Cape Cod, Mass.

MARINES EMBARK FOR NEAR EAST TROUBLE SPOT

As the threat of war looms in the Near and Middle East, the Second Battalion of the Eighth Marines embarks for the Mediterranean on six ships of the Atlantic Fleet.

Even as the Marines leave, new violence erupts in Cyprus, North Africa and Palestine.

The Marines head for the trouble spot and Americans hope they don't have to land.

WAR OVER SUEZ

In a dramatic sequence of events, the Suez Canal, lifeline of Europe, becomes a cause of war.

JUNE	**B**ritain ends 72-year occupation of the Suez Canal Zone.
JULY	**E**gypt's President Nasser announces nationalization of the Suez Canal Company—seizing full control of the Canal.
AUGUST	**U**.S., France and Great Britain hold discussions on the Suez Canal. Great Britain mobilizes forces.
	Egypt announces willingness to discuss the Suez only after Great Britain and France pull out.
	Nasser agrees to five-nation mission to discuss the Suez.
	Britain grants France permission to station troops on Cyprus.
SEPTEMBER	**E**gypt assumes full control of Suez Canal using all Egyptian employees—war threatened.
OCTOBER	**15** member nations formally inaugurate Suez Canal Users Association.
	Morocco and Tunisia recall their ambassadors to France in protest over action in the Suez.
	President Eisenhower assures nation that U.S. will not get involved in Middle East hostilities.
	Britain, France and Israel move on Suez Canal. French and British planes bomb Egyptian airport and military installations near Suez. President Nasser vows Egypt will fight any foreign intervention.
NOVEMBER	**I**sraeli troops capture Gaza strip, seizing control of Sinai. Golda Meir claims Gaza strip is part of Israel.
	In an overwhelming majority (65-1), U.N. Assembly calls for withdrawal of foreign forces.
	Suez operation ends after intense pressure from the United Nations.
DECEMBER	**B**ritish and French troops evacuate from the Suez.

President Abdel Nasser announces seizure of the canal by Egypt.

Israeli troops strike down the Sinai Peninsula to within a few miles of the Canal and within days Egyptian troops are completely routed.

Britain and France stage a joint sea and air invasion.

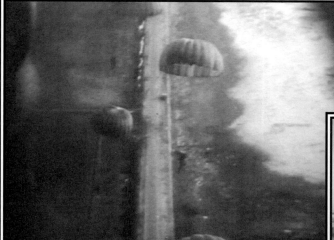

Airborne troops quickly follow and establish a beachhead at the entrance to the Canal.

The debris and chaos of bombing greet the Anglo-French forces as they enter the conquered cities.

To implement the decision, Secretary General Dag Hammarskjold flies to Egypt for preliminary negotiations.

The police force is jubilantly welcomed as it takes up its task in Egypt.

As the occupation proceeds, world opinion against the invasion is mobilized. At the United Nations, the invasion is branded "aggression" and a ceasefire is ordered.

The United Nations emergency police force is born.

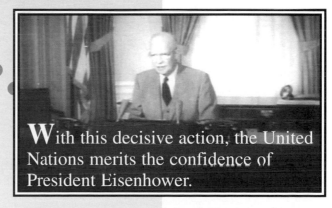

With this decisive action, the United Nations merits the confidence of President Eisenhower.

"In the past, the United Nations has proved able to find a way to end bloodshed. We believe it can and that it will do so again."

IT'S A LANDSLIDE
EISENHOWER/NIXON

DAILY

Adlai Stevenson, former governor of Illinois, becomes the standard bearer for the Democratic party at its convention in Chicago.

The Republican convention meets in San Francisco and their choice by overwhelming acclamation is President Eisenhower.

WHAT A YEAR IT WAS!

FOR TICKET

CIRCULATION 3

Republican supporters gather in Times Square to await election returns.

Jubilant Eisenhower and Nixon greet their supporters in this historic election—the biggest landslide victory since Franklin D. Roosevelt beat Alfred M. Landon in 1936.

1956

Governors Of Georgia, Mississippi, South Carolina And Virginia United In Opposition Of Supreme Court's Ban On Racial Segregation In Public Schools. Virginia Supports Segregation By Funding Private Schools.

Despite An Angry, Hostile Mob, Autherine Lucy Becomes First Negro* To Be Admitted To The University Of Alabama. The University Then Votes To Suspend Her Because Of Demonstrations Over Her Admission. She Is Later Expelled Because Of Charges She Made Against The University.

115 People Indicted By Montgomery, Alabama Grand Jury For Alleged Involvement In 11-Week Boycott Of Bus System.

U.S. Supreme Court Affirms Ban On Segregated Public Schools.

University of Florida Ordered By Supreme Court To Admit Negro* Student To Its Law School.

Martin Luther King, Jr. Convicted In Montgomery, Alabama State Court On Charges of Illegally Conspiring To Boycott Segregated Buses.

Segregation Of Public Transportation Declared Unconstitutional By U.S. Supreme Court.

Alabama State Court Bars The NAACP.

Tennessee National Guard Called In To Stop Riots Over Admission Of l2 Negro* Children in Clinton—Nine Students Admitted.

Students Seeking To Attend An Integrated High School In Sturgis, Kentucky, Have The Way Cleared For Them By National Guard Soldiers With Fixed Bayonets.

*Negro was the commonly used term in 1956.

26

WHAT A YEAR IT WAS!

HUNGARY'S VALIANT FIGHT FOR FREEDOM

Emblems of Red tyranny come down for 10 glorious days as Hungarian patriots struggle against 20 Russian armored divisions.

The struggle pits raw courage and rifles against tanks.

Hungary's

The taste of freedom is brief as 120,000 Hungarians flee to the Austrian border to escape Russian tanks, leaving up to 25,000 patriots dead.

Rebellion

February

October

- U.S. Government Reimposes Ban On U.S. Travel To Hungary.

- Anti-Soviet Protests Turn Into Full-Scale War In Hungary. Police Open Fire On Students.
- Premier Nagy Launches Attack To Quell Revolt. Mass Burial Held For Slain Students And Workers.
- The United States, France And Great Britain Protest Soviet Intervention.
- Cardinal Mindszenty Set Free In Budapest.

November

- Premier Nagy Renounces Warsaw Pact As Soviet Troops Take Over Budapest.
- Premier Nagy Arrested As Soviets Invade Budapest With 1,000 Tanks.
- Hungarian Patriot Drapes Hungarian Flag On Statue Of Liberty.
- Soviet Tanks Brutally Crush Budapest Revolt—Up To 25,000 Hungarians Killed And 30,000 Wounded.
- Soviet Tanks Open Fire On U.S. Embassy.
- Jean Paul Sartre, French Philosopher And Novelist, Splits With Communist Party Over Its Brutality In Handling The Hungarian Rebellion.
- Nine Member Countries Of The U.N. Security Council, Including Communist Yugoslavia, Approve American Resolution Censuring The Soviet Union.

December

- U.S. Opens Door To 21,500 More Hungarian Refugees.
- Communist Hardliner, Janos Kadar, Tries To Include Moderates in Coalition Government.
- Former Premier Imre Nagy Holds Position On Supporting Free Elections.
- Protesting Soviet Occupation, Strikes And Slowdowns Paralyze Hungarian Industry.
- U.N. Calls For Immediate Withdrawal Of Soviet Troops From Hungary.

WHAT A YEAR IT WAS!

❖ Fidel Castro, Exiled Student Leader, Accused Of Leading Cuban Rebels In Uprising.

❖ Sudan Proclaimed Independent Republic.

❖ Islam Becomes State Religion Of Egypt.

❖ First National Assembly Election Held In Viet Nam With Pro-West Diem Regime Winning.

❖ Socialist Guy Mollet Becomes French Premier.

❖ The 20th Congress Of The Communist Party Of The Soviet Union Officially Signals End of Stalinism And Return To Leninism.

❖ Tunisia Abolishes Polygamy, Amends Divorce Laws In Favor Of Wives And Grants Voting Rights To Women Over 21.

❖ Pakistan Becomes First Islamic Republic.

❖ Stalin Denounced By Khrushchev—Reforms Begin In U.S.S.R.

❖ West Germany Bans Communist Party And Reinstates Military Service.

❖ President of Nicaragua, General Anastasio Somoza, Victim Of Assassin's Bullet.

❖ Luis A. Somoza Elected President of Nicaragua, Succeeding His Father, Anastasio.

❖ Somalia Holds First National Elections.

❖ Golda Meir Replaces Moshe Sharett As Foreign Minister Of Israel.

❖ Egyptian President Nasser Proclaims End Of Martial Law And Censorship Of The Press In Effect Since The Overthrow Of King Farouk In 1952.

❖ King Mahendra, The World's Only Hindu Monarch, Is Crowned In Nepal.

❖ Japan And USSR End State Of War.

❖ Mutual Defense Pact Against Israel Signed By Syria And Lebanon.

❖ France Grants Independence To Its Two Protectorates In North Africa—Tunisia And Morocco.

EGYPT PARADES ITS ARSENAL OF RED WEAPONS

Egypt flexes its military muscle with a display of arms newly acquired from Russia and its satellites.

The parade, which climaxes a 3-day celebration of the withdrawal of the last British troops from the Suez, is presided over by newly elected president Abdel Nasser, spearhead of the Arab bloc of nations.

Russia's new foreign minister, Dmitri Shepilov, architect of the arms deal, observes the proceedings.

U.N. Secretary General Dag Hammarskjold Reports Israeli-Egyptian Cease-Fire Agreement.

The Soviet Union Releases Poland's Wladyslaw Gomulka And Restores The Polish Army.

Battle For Algiers Begins.

Eisenhower Rejects Soviets' Proposed 20-Year Treaty Of Friendship. Soviet Premier Bulganin Urges Ike to Reconsider.

Vice-President Nixon Delivers Letter From President Eisenhower To Generalissimo Chiang Kai-shek Confirming U.S. Support Of Nationalist China.

Eisenhower Issues Statement Reaffirming U.S. Friendship With Great Britain And France.

Douglas MacArthur II Named U.S. Ambassador To Japan.

• PASSINGS •

Alben Barkley,
U.S. Vice President 1949-1953,
dies at 78.

870 TWO-DOOR CATALINA

860 TWO-DOOR CATALINA

STAR CHIEF TWO-DOOR CATALINA

Pontiac Covers The Field

Meet America's "first family" of hardtops—six gorgeous two- and four-door models, Catalina styled as only Pontiac can do it.

What a field to choose from: three price ranges, two wheelbases, two horsepower options and so wide a variety of colors and fabrics that virtually the only limit on your choice is your own imagination!

Here are cars that beg for action in every long, sleek, luxurious line! When you give them the nod to go—*they* go—like no car has ever gone before! You feel the instant surge of 227 blaz-

THE CAR SAYS "GO" AND THE PRICE WON'T STOP YOU!

34

870 FOUR-DOOR CATALINA

860 FOUR-DOOR CATALINA

STAR CHIEF FOUR-DOOR CATALINA

With Hardtops

ing horsepower—smoothed almost beyond belief by Pontiac's exclusive Strato-Flight Hydra-Matic*.

While you're thrilling to the greatest "go" on wheels, you're relaxing in the solid comfort of Pontiac's spacious interiors, extra-long wheelbase and cradled ride. You enjoy, too, the safety of Pontiac's rugged construction and easy handling.

So when you're caught by the hardtop mood—and it likely will be soon—pay us a visit. You'll find exactly the car you want—at exactly the price you want to pay. *An extra-cost option.*

'56 STRATO-STREAK

PONTIAC

SEE YOUR PONTIAC DEALER

35

PEOPLE

QUEEN ELIZABETH WELCOMED IN NIGERIA

Gaily bedecked natives dressed in their finest await the arrival of Queen Elizabeth, the first reigning sovereign to visit the century-old West African crown colony.

WHAT A YEAR IT WAS!

Her Majesty and the Duke of Edinburgh are greeted by the Governor General and other government officials.

A highlight of the welcoming ceremony is the presentation of a bouquet of flowers by a beautiful 4-year old child.

WHAT A YEAR IT WAS!

Happy Birthday, Queen Mum

Britain's Favorite Mum, Queen Mother Elizabeth Turns 56.

A Hot Time In The Old House Tonight

Sir Winston Churchill awoke after a good night's sleep to learn that he had slept right through a small fire that erupted in his kitchen just a few steps away from his bedroom.

Duchess Of Windsor's Autobiography, "The Heart Has Its Reasons" Serialized In McCall's.

Anthony Eden And Clement Attlee Become Knights Of The Order Of The Garter.

Agatha Christie, Margot Fonteyn And Sir Osbert Sitwell Honored By Queen Elizabeth For Their Services To The Crown.

- **Former President Harry S. Truman Awarded Honorary Degree At Oxford.**

- **President Truman's advice on the proper attire to wear for his daughter Margaret's upcoming wedding to dashing Clifton Daniel?** *"The best pair of pants you've got, and just so long as you're covered up you'll be in style!"*

TOASTING THE HOST THE MOST

In an impressive display of drinking prowess at a reception held at the Danish Embassy, Russia's Premier Nikolai Bulganin imbibed 20 martinis in an hour-and-a-half of toasting to a broad range of subjects.

Treat yourself to beer

that stays COOL

<u>*93% longer*</u>

Look for the words:
NO DEPOSIT
NO RETURN

in <u>NEW</u> **QUART BOTTLES** *you don't return*

Let your own taste prove what scientists have confirmed in the laboratory.

Beer or ale in the new Party-Size Quart Bottle has it all over other nonreturnable containers . . . for cold-retention, for lip-smacking flavor. For instance, these big Party Quart Bottles keep your favorite brand *cool 93% longer* than 12-ounce cans. It's easy to make the test yourself.

Glass pampers the flavor peak of fine beers and ales.

Prove this, too. Just let your favorite beer or ale aerate freely down the neck of the bottle, over the bottle's clean lip, straight into a glass. Let it form its natural head. The first refreshing sip tells you how important a bottle is to beer's protection . . . how important the neck of a bottle is to beer's flavor.

Party-Size Quart Bottles are the "life" of the party.

—5 glasses of your favorite beer at its best. If you are like most hosts, the big new Party-Size Quart Bottle will be your favorite for serving guests because it keeps beer within the just-right 40- to 50-degree temperature range far longer than when each guest has a separate small container.

Pilsner illustrated is from Libbey's smartly styled Royal Fern line.

Serve these PARTY-SIZE GLASS BOTTLES this weekend – *you <u>don't</u> have to take 'em back!*

NO DEPOSIT—NO RETURN BOTTLES
AN (I) PRODUCT

OWENS-ILLINOIS
GENERAL OFFICES · TOLEDO 1, OHIO

39

Happy Birthday, Pope

Catholics of the world rejoice on the 80th birthday of Pope Pius XII and the complete recovery of his health.

1956 marks the 17th year of the pontiff's reign, a religious milestone.

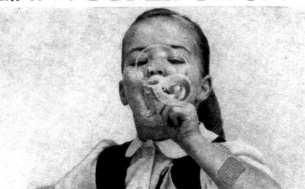
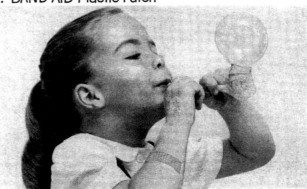
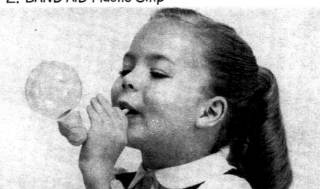
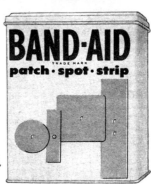

IRISH PRIME MINISTER VISITS WASHINGTON

John A. Costello, the first Prime Minister of Ireland ever to visit the United States, arrives in Washington for a state visit.

The Prime Minister receives a warm welcome from Vice President Richard Nixon and Undersecretary of State Herbert Hoover, Jr.

A hearty welcome from President Eisenhower, who will play host to Prime Minister Costello whose visit corresponds with St. Patrick's Day.

* Howard Hughes Receives Eviction Notice From The City Of Long Beach, California To Remove His Experimental Flying Boat, The Hercules, Which Has Been In Storage Since 1947.

* FBI Director, J. Edgar Hoover, Declares The Word "Cop" Unfavorable, Requesting Use Of A More Respectful Term—Police Officer.

* Roving U.P. Columnist Gloria Swanson Congratulates Grace Kelly On Making The Flat Chested Look Both Fashionable And Desirable.

* Jayne Mansfield Named Miss Negligee Of 1956 By Underwear-Negligee Associates Convention In Manhattan.

* Sweden's Sultry Actress Anita Ekberg Loses The Upper Portion Of Her Skin-Tight Strapless Gown In Posh London Hotel. Major Fallout!

GEORGE NADER RECEIVES NAVY AWARD

1,000 Navy men and more than 100 movie critics and writers gather at a special screening at the Brooklyn Navy Yard to see George Nader receive a U.S. Navy citation for his performance in the new movie "Away All Boats."

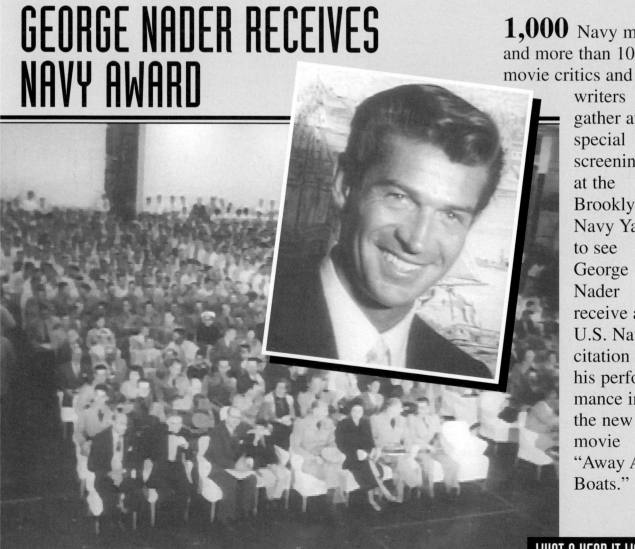

ROSES FOR MISS BORCHERS

Actress Cornell Borchers arrives in the United States to receive recognition for her work in "Divided Heart."

The German actress makes her American debut this year with Rock Hudson in "Never Say Goodbye."

IT'S ENOUGH TO MAKE YOU SIT DOWN AND CRY

Johnnie Ray Almost Loses His Shirt As Adoring Teen-Age Fans Rip His Clothes After Breaking Through Barricades In Sydney, Australia.

A Blushing Marlon Brando Is Left Stammering As 100 Filipino Bobby-Soxers With Raging Hormones Crash His News Conference To Get A Look At The American Movie Star.

The Most Admired Women

Eleanor Roosevelt
(10th time in 11 years)
Clare Boothe Luce
Mamie Eisenhower
Helen Keller
Queen Elizabeth II
Princess Margaret
Senator Margaret Chase Smith
Madame Chiang Kai-shek
Madame Vijaya Lakshmi Pandit

MAMIE EISENHOWER WELCOMES
Mother of the Year

Mamie Eisenhower welcomes members of the Mother of the Year Committee.

The First Lady chats with honoree, Mrs. Jane Maxwell Pritchard, who was awarded the signal honor for 1956.

◇ Frank Costello Begins 5-Year Jail Sentence For Income Tax Evasion.

◇ Labor Racketeer Johnny Dioguardia Arrested Along With Four Others In Acid-Throwing Attack Blinding Of Columnist Victor Riesel.

◇ Tokyo Rose Is Released From Prison After Serving Her Sentence For Committing Treasonable Acts During World War II.

◇ Playwright Clifford Odets Jailed For Drunken Driving After Leaving Scene Of Accident.

◇ Mail-Order Heir Montgomery Ward Thorne Is Found Dead In Chicago Slum After Apparent Sex-And-Drug Orgy.

◇ The Great John Barrymore's Daughter, Diana, Checks Into A Sanitarium For Her Drinking Problem.

WHAT A YEAR IT WAS!

★ Broadway Stars Pay Tribute To Helen Hayes On The 50th Anniversary Of Her First Stage Appearance.

★ After A 16-Year Fight With Alcoholism, Lillian Roth Gets Rave Reviews For Her Performance At New York's Hotel Plaza.

★ Jackie Robinson Receives NAACP's Spingarn Medal For Highest Achievement By An American Negro.*

*Negro was the commonly used term in 1956.

★ President Eisenhower Appoints William Joseph Brennan, Jr. Associate Justice Of The U.S. Supreme Court.

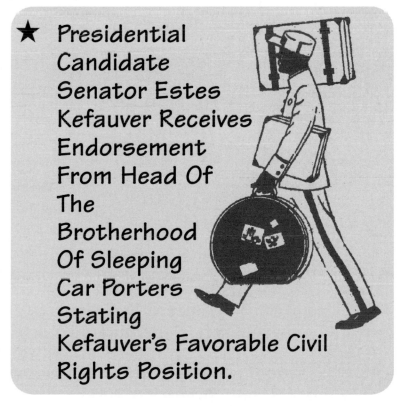

★ Presidential Candidate Senator Estes Kefauver Receives Endorsement From Head Of The Brotherhood Of Sleeping Car Porters Stating Kefauver's Favorable Civil Rights Position.

WHAT A YEAR IT WAS!

Couplings

Willie Mays &
Marghuerite Wendelle

Efrem Zimbalist Jr. &
Loranda Stephanie Spalding

Terry Moore & Eugene McGrath

Polly Bergen & Freddie Fields

Aldous Huxley & Laura Achera

Julius La Rosa & Rosemary Meyer

Audrey Meadows & Randolph Rouse

Dave Garroway &
Pamela Wilde Kastner de Coninck

Shirley Jones & Jack Cassidy

Leslie Caron & Peter Hall

Carol Channing &
Charles Franklin Lowe

Sharon Kay Ritchie & Don Cherry

Gregory Peck & Veronique Passani

UnCouplings

Ruth Roman & Mortimer W. Hall

Alfred Gwynne Vanderbilt &
Jeanne Lourdes Murray Vanderbilt

Tyrus (Ty) Cobb &
Frances Fairbairn Cass Cobb

Sonja Henie &
William Gardiner

Elizabeth Taylor &
Michael Wilding

Sammy Kaye &
Ruth Kaye

Marie McDonald &
Harry Karl

Edward G. Robinson &
Mrs. Edward G. Robinson

Jeanne Crain & Paul Brinkman

Vivian Blaine & Manny G. Frank

Divorced Or Not Divorced—That Is The Question

John Jacob Astor thought he had divorced his wife, Mrs. Gertrude Gretsch Astor in Mexico and proceeded to marry Dolores Fullman when lo and behold, the New York Supreme Court held the divorce invalid and granted a separation instead. In the meantime, John separated from Dolores which translates into being separated from not one but two wives. Keep that checkbook handy, John.

WHAT A YEAR IT WAS!

NEW *REO* MOWS ANY LAWN IN ONE CLEAN SWEEP

and you don't have to push!

Now you can give your entire lawn a neat, clipped, brushed look *with a mower that travels on its own power!*

The new Reo Power-Trim cuts grass beautifully, trims close, mulches leaves, chops weeds . . . and all *you* do is steer. It drives itself along at a normal walking speed. Takes grades in stride. Does the heavy work when you have to plow through high grass or weeds. Helps you finish faster—and fresher!

What's more, Reo's Front Wheel Drive gives you better *control* at all times. To turn or maneuver, just press down on the mower handle—driving wheels lift from ground. For really close trimming, just shift to neutral—mower becomes free-wheeling. Easy? Even the little woman can run it!

You can set blade at any of 4 cutting heights in seconds—without tools, without removing wheels. 21-inch model has an extra Creeper speed for heavy going in overgrown areas. Both models are powered by a rugged Reo 2¼ hp. 4-cycle easy-starting engine that runs on regular gas. Don't push a mower any more. Get behind a new Reo Power-Trim!

Exclusive Reo Design saves raking and sweeping. Reo Suction-Lift Blade is enclosed like a ducted fan. Strong suction pulls grass up for even cut, sprays the clippings out. Reo Triple Duty Door adjusts mower for any grass-cutting condition:

WIDE-OPEN for longest grass and weeds. Cuttings are shot out, away from mower. No clogging.

TOP OPEN for regularly mowed lawns. Clippings are spread out *evenly*. No windrows to rake.

CLOSED for fine-mulching of grass or leaves. Tiny mulched particles sift *into* lawn. No sweeping.

18-inch model, $149.95*   **2-speed 21-inch model, $169.95***

Other Reo Rotaries with same lawn-grooming features start at **$89.95***. Write for name of your nearest Reo Dealer in the U.S. or Canada. *Slightly higher in West and Canada.

More than a million people mow with Reo

The greatest name in POWER MOWERS
Sold and Serviced Everywhere

Product of Motor Wheel Corporation • Lansing 3, Michigan, U.S.A.

COPYRIGHT 1956 BY MOTOR WHEEL CORP.

LEVELS TALL GRASS AND WEEDS

MULCHES LEAVES INTO LAWN

SAVES HAND-CLIPPING AND EDGE-TRIMMING

TRIMS WITHIN ³/₈-INCH OF TREES, WALLS, FENCES

CUTS SO FINE, CLIPPINGS DISAPPEAR

A MOVIE QUEEN SAILS OFF TO BECOME A PRINCESS

Surrounded by well-wishers and the press, Grace Kelly gets ready to board the S.S. Constitution for her trip to Monaco.

America wishes Grace bon voyage and a lifetime of happiness.

WHAT A YEAR IT WAS!

THE WORLD'S MOST ELIGIBLE BACHELOR TAKES A BRIDE

All the world focuses on the tiny kingdom of Monaco as this storybook country prepares for Prince Rainier's marriage to American film queen Grace Kelly.

A wildly enthusiastic crowd gathers to greet the ship carrying the soon-to-be Princess Grace.

Prince Rainier III kneels next to Grace Patricia Kelly in the Roman Catholic St. Nicholas Cathedral in Monte Carlo after a civil ceremony the day before.

The wedding festivities were covered by 1,700 press, radio, TV and newsreel reporters and photographers from Western Europe and the United States.

1956

HONEYMOONERS PRINCE RAINIER AND PRINCESS GRACE ATTEND A BULLFIGHT

The Prince and his famous movie queen bride make their way to their box for a day at the bullfights.

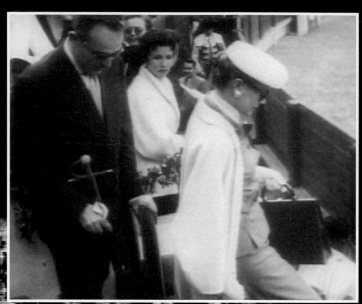

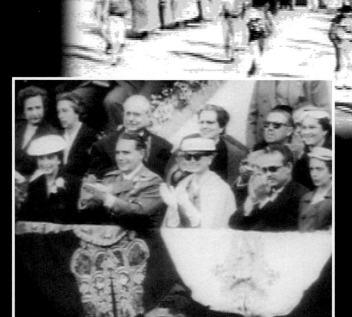

The festivities begin with the traditional grand march of the matadors and picadors.

The opening ceremony receives royal approval.

Princess Grace is moved by the action in the ring as the bull gores the horse.

A triumphant matador tosses his hat to the most beautiful woman in the arena who responds to a gallant victory by returning his hat.

• **Romano Mussolini, Il Duce's Youngest Son, Makes His Jazz Piano Debut At San Remo's International Jazz Festival.**

• **White Dove Soup Cures Madame Chiang Kai-shek's Skin Rash.**

A CROSS EXCHANGE

Defending accusations by a group of Australian preachers who called him a fraud and an imposter and insisted that he leave the country immediately, the flamboyant and prosperous Rev. Oral Roberts insisted that he was a child of God and that Christ had no objections to prosperity.

EVERYTHING YOU EVER NEEDED TO KNOW....

Stunned by announcement by their children's school, Washington's Sidwell Friends School, that they would be admitting a number of qualified Negro* students to their kindergarten class, avid segregationists Senator and Mrs. James O. Eastland consoled themselves by the fact that since their children had already completed kindergarten, it was unlikely that they would have any Negro* classmates.

Negro was the commonly accepted term in 1956.

• **Ed Sullivan Suffers Injuries In Head-On Car Crash.**

• **Actor Kirk Douglas Sues Walt Disney And ABC For Invasion Of Privacy, Charging Home Movies Shot In Disney's Home During A Social Visit Were Shown On Television Without His Consent.**

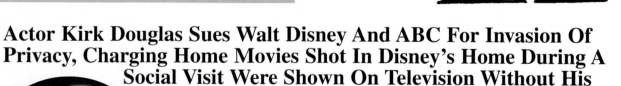

• **Dean Martin & Jerry Lewis End Their 10-Year Partnership.**

• **Marilyn Monroe Marries Playwright Arthur Miller In London.**

Plenty of zoom at the top

IT HAPPENS right at the top of gas pedal travel.

Your foot goes down—maybe less than an inch—and Dynaflow Drive* comes up with a spang-new getaway that opens your eyes.

Suppose, for example, you want to enter the stream of traffic—or change your lane—or alter course.

Whatever you want to do, a bare touch of your toe achieves it. With sure confidence. With greater safety than ever before.

And light-footing the treadle like this, you save a pretty penny on gasoline in the bargain.

But that's not the whole of it. Not by a long shot!

For there's still *another*, still a *greater* take-off waiting for your call. It's the full-power switch-pitch breakaway you get by pressing the pedal all the way down.

It's like the giant hand of a friendly genie whisking you out of trouble. And brother, it's a boon just knowing it's there.

This is truly something you deserve to enjoy . . .

The thrill of command behind a big 322-cubic-inch Buick V8 engine—so brimful of live power that at 50 m.p.h., nine-tenths of its potential remains in reserve . . .

The feel of a lithe-handling, lighthearted and luxurious Buick—a suavely styled and beautifully engineered Buick—a 1956 Buick that's the blue-ribbon best of a true-blooded breed.

Actually, it's almost easier done than said. We have a demonstration car on the ready line if you have a few minutes to match it.

So why hold back? Drop in this week and start things moving!

New Advanced Variable Pitch Dynaflow is the only Dynaflow Buick builds today. It is standard on Roadmaster, Super and Century—optional at modest extra cost on the Special.
†*Standard on Roadmaster and Super, optional at extra cost on other Series.*

NEW Precision-Balanced Chassis, engineered all new from front to rear for extra-rugged roadability

NEW V8 Power Peaks in Every Buick

NEW Variable Pitch Dynaflow*— with double-action take-off

NEW Deep-Oil-Cushioned Luxury Ride—with all-coil springing and true torque-tube drive

NEW Sweep-Ahead Styling— with Fashion Color Harmony inside and out

NEW Smoother-Action Brakes with Suspended Pedal

NEW Stepped-up Gas Mileage in All Buicks

NEW Safety Power Steering†— for instant and constant response

—and 97 Other New Features

SEE JACKIE GLEASON ON TV— Every Saturday Evening

When better automobiles are built Buick will build them

See Your Buick Dealer

53

HUMAN INTEREST

HOSPITAL MOVE:
Trucks Transfer 300 Patients In Two Hours

In Evansville, Indiana, Operation Good Neighbor aids in the evacuation of St. Mary's Hospital with 110 pieces of rolling stock taking part in the transfer of the patients, beds and all.

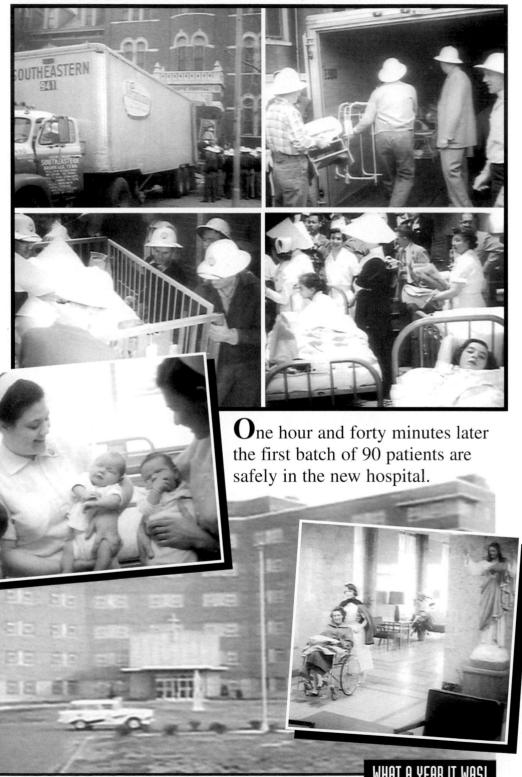

Patients are carefully loaded into tractor vans attended by nuns and nurses for the 7-mile trip to the new building.

One hour and forty minutes later the first batch of 90 patients are safely in the new hospital.

WHAT A YEAR IT WAS!

Harvard To Raise Tuition $200, Increasing The College Cost To $1,000 And $1,200 For The Business School.

New York Coliseum Opens.

The First Climate-Controlled Shopping Center Opens Outside Of Minneapolis, Attracting Over 40,000 Potential Customers.

Margaret E. Towner Becomes The First Woman To Be Ordained As A Minister By The Presbyterian Church In Syracuse, New York.

Perry H. Young Becomes The First Negro* Crew Member On An American Airline On Being Hired By A Helicopter Company, New York Airways.

"**D**ear Abby" Makes Its Debut For The McNaught Syndicate.

U.S. Army Gets Its First Official Flag.

Columbus, Ohio Zoo Reports First Gorilla Born In Captivity.

U.S. Postal Service Issues First Stamp Designed To Emphasize Importance Of Wildlife Conservation.

*Negro was the commonly used term in 1956.

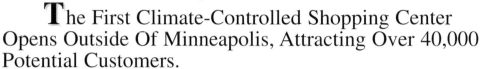

YOU WANT ME TO SAY HOW MANY HAIL MARYS??

Angered by his priest, and guided by an inner voice, a young Englishman threw open the door of his confessional and punched the priest in the eye.

A BOX-OFFICE FLOP

A Los Angeles thief with a flair for the dramatic, walked up to a movie box office, whipped out a gun and demanded everyone's money back on the grounds that he didn't like the film.

WHAT A YEAR IT WAS!

1956

MANEUVERS AT 40 BELOW ZERO

NORTH POLE 802 MILES

FORT BRAGG, N.C. HOME OF 82ND AIRBORNE 3500 MILES

Burdened by parachutes and bulky parkas, 700 paratroopers board their planes in Greenland for Exercise Arctic Night.

The 82nd Airborne makes their jump, landing on a frozen fjord with a layer of ice 55 inches thick.

The paratroopers dig snow shelters to keep warm.

LEADING BRITISH SEXOLOGIST DISPENSES BEDROOM ADVICE FOR MARRIED COUPLES AS FOLLOWS:

- Separate bedrooms for the husband and wife, his for general use and hers for romantic evenings;
- The head of the bed should face north or south;
- The woman should wear a long, flowing silk nightgown with a lace top;
- Never, ever have twin beds as that is the quickest way to end marital bliss.

TO TIE THE KNOT OR NOT TO TIE THE KNOT — RECENT STUDY REVEALS FAVORITE REASONS FOR MARRYING

- Security
- Independence From Parents
- Having Someone Who Cares
- Procreation
- Sexual Satisfaction
- Sharing Common Interests

TILL DEATH DO US PART OR WE DIVORCE— WHICHEVER COMES FIRST

- An Increasing Number Of Women Resume Their Maiden Names After Divorce.
- Alimony Granted In Less Than 3% Of Divorces.
- Highest Rate Of Divorce Is In Fifth Year Of Marriage.
- Divorce Rate Higher Among Women With Previous Marriages Or Who Were Pregnant Before They Married.

TOTAL U.S. POPULATION:
169,000,000

COUPLING & UNCOUPLING
NUMBER OF MARRIAGES:1,585,000
NUMBER OF DIVORCES: 382,000

ARRIVALS
NUMBER OF BIRTHS: 4,210,000

59

NEW WORDS

ACCOMMODATION SALE
The sale of a commodity to another dealer for resale.

AFTERBURNER
A device for burning gas that passes through to the exhaust pipe of an automobile.

AWARDEE
To give (one) an award.

BRANE
Bombing Radar Navigation Equipment—an electronic device to direct an airplane to its target with great accuracy.

BRINKMANSHIP
The practice, especially in international politics, of seeking advantage by creating the impression that one is willing and able to pass the brink of nuclear war rather than concede.

BARGANZA:

A bargain sale, or a group of bargains.

CANYONEER
One who runs western rivers in various types of small boats.

EURATOM
European Atomic Pool.

FRONTAGE ROAD
On a limited access highway, a turnout road usually for a filling station or restaurant.

GREYLISTED
Partly, not completely, blacklisted.

MISSILRY
Guided missiles considered collectively.

MORTGAGE WAREHOUSING
The use of commercial bank credit on an interim basis by mortgage lenders.

MOTELERY
A huge, luxurious hotel designed for leisurely modern living, with some of the advantages of motels.

NEW WORDS

ORPHAN VIRUS
An unidentified virus.

PENTAMIC ARMY
A U.S. army fighting force with five battle groups to a division.

RAMPED STAGE
A stage sloping up at the rear to give better perspective.

ROLL ON, ROLL OFF
The system of shipping via water in which large loaded crates, trucks and railroad cars are rolled onto a ship at a port and rolled off at another.

ROLLOUT
The rolling of an airplane from a production line.

SEW-OFF
A final contest among home seamstresses.

SPLIT-TIME
A daylight saving time using a half hour rather than an hour advance.

STEEL BAND
A musical band, usually calypso, using oil drums.

STORM TRACKER
A device for gathering weather data.

TEAR-AWAY JERSEY
A football jersey that tears easily and cannot be used to keep a player from running when grasped by an opponent.

WINE-MOBILE
An automobile that dispenses wines.

ZIGZAG EATING:

Shifting one's fork to the other hand.

Family Affairs

A recent study conducted by a domestic relations expert revealed that while children can sometimes hold a marriage together, they can also contribute to its break-up, while another study showed that children of broken marriages were better adjusted than children of parents who were unhappily married.

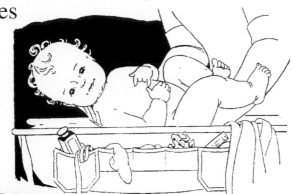

❖ **Couples In Their Fifties Become Closer To Their Spouses And Get New Enjoyment Out Of Life After Their Children Leave Home.**

❖ **Resolution Opposing Interfaith Marriages As A Threat To The Faith Of The Catholic Spouse And Religious Training Of The Children Is Adopted By The National Catholic Family Life Convention.**

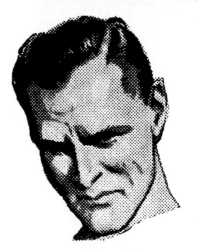

MARRIED MEN GET POOR PRESS IN THE COMICS

A New York University professor made the following observation with respect to how married men are depicted in comic strips:

☞ HIS WIFE'S SCAPEGOAT   ☞ HIS CHILDREN'S DUPE

☞ WISHY-WASHY BUNGLER   ☞ UNDEPENDABLE IN TIMES OF CRISIS

☞ CONTINUALLY FRUSTRATED   ☞ GENERALLY INFERIOR TO HIS WIFE

SINGLE MEN, ON THE OTHER HAND, ARE SHOWN TO BE EXTREMELY MASCULINE AND DOMINATE BEAUTIFUL, BUT DEPENDENT, WOMEN.

The biggest dry land regatta in history is launched as the National Motorboat Show opens in New York.

National MOTORBOAT SHOW

With an increasing number of Americans involved in boating, outboard motors attract a great deal of attention.

The show features every nautical need from this $11,000 outboard beauty to a $50 home assembly pram to a luxury cruiser priced in excess of $100,000.

FAVORITES WITH THE SUN SET !

The powder that *Chafe-Guards*... There's nothing like a cool sprinkling of Johnson's Baby Powder to smooth away chafes and prickles ... keep baby's skin comfy, fresh, fragrant. Because only Johnson's contains a *Chafe-Guard* ingredient that *neutralizes* irritants in body moisture.

The oil that *Safe-Guards*... And there's no finer protection against the drying effects of sun and wind than Johnson's Baby Oil — America's favorite way to keep skin baby-soft and smooth. Because pure, soothing Johnson's helps Safe-Guard the *natural* oils in delicate skin.

Johnson&Johnson

Johnson's
BABY
OIL
Johnson&Johnson

Johnson's
BABY
POWDER
Johnson&Johnson

Milwaukee Housewife Sues Her Husband For Divorce On The Grounds He Keeps Singing The Same Song Over And Over — *"I Wish I Were Single Again."*

○ A Cleveland Woman Sued Her House Painter After He Painted Her Arm Red When She Criticized The Quality Of His Work.

○ Women In Their Thirties Return To The Workforce, Finding Even The Most Menial Jobs More Stimulating Than Staying At Home.

○ Women With Higher Education Have Fewer Children Than Their Less Educated Counterparts.

○ Under A New Social Security Amendment, Women Would Become Eligible For Benefits At 62 Instead Of 65.

SOMETHING TO BARK ABOUT

The Westminster Kennel Club of New York took a historic step by awarding Mrs. Bertha Smith's 6-lb. white toy poodle, Wilber White Swan, top honors. This was the first time a toy breed became champion.

Grey Squirrels Destroy Half-Million Dollars' Worth Of U.S. Telephone Cable Yearly— Bell Labs Suspend Costly Research, Stating Failure To Come Up With An Effective Deterrent.

Legendary Himalayan Abominable Snowman Footprints Spotted In French Alpine Resort Of Val-d'Isère.

• Ringling Bros. And Barnum And Bailey Circus Holds Its Last Performance Under A Tent, Opting To Switch To Large Indoor Venues.

• Philadelphia Court Engages In Unprecedented Experiment And Allows Press Photographer Inside Courtroom.

• Colorado Becomes First State To Allow Courtroom Coverage By Photographers, As Well As Radio And Television Reporters.

• The Automobile Ferry Ceases Operation In San Francisco Bay On Opening Of Richmond-San Rafael Bridge —The World's Second Longest High-Level Crossing.

hardware, dry goods

66

p Value Stamps
REDEMPTION STORE

1956

HERE'S LOOKING AT YOU, KID
OR
THE LOOK OF........IS IN YOUR EYES

A New York psychiatrist explored the hidden meaning behind a variety of looks and came to the following conclusions:

KIND OF LOOK	MEANING
Excessive Blinking	Reality Avoidance
Fixed, Depressed Gaze	Need Of Consolation
Dramatic Gaze	A Cover For Inner Conflicts And Inferiority Complex
Absent Gaze	Defense Against People
Averted Gaze	Avoidance of Feelings And Responsibilities

★ Aviation Safety Record Set For Domestic Commercial Airlines.

★ U.S. Navy Icebreaker Reports Antarctic Iceberg Twice The Size Of Connecticut.

★ Swiss Expedition Scales Mt. Everest And Is The First To Climb Lhotse.

★ Kashmir's Mt. Gasherbrum, Second Highest Unclimbed Mountain, Scaled By Austrian Team Led By Fritz Moravec.

★ U.S. Consumption Of Newsprint Reaches All-Time High Despite Severe Paper Shortage.

★ The FBI Reports More Major Crimes Committed In 1956 Than In Any Other Year.

★ College Age Population Lowest In 25 Years.

★ Membership In 4-H Clubs Reaches Record High.

★ Gasoline Rationing Returns To Great Britain.

★ Post-War Airplane Passenger Travel Increases Dramatically, Matching Number Of Train Passengers.

★ 840,000 Students Deprived Of Full-Time Classroom Instruction Due To Teacher/Classroom Shortage.

★ Suburban Housing Boom Sweeps America.

WHAT A YEAR IT WAS!

On The Horns Of Being A

Female Teenager

THE MOST COMMON QUESTIONS

- *Should you kiss a boy on the first date?*
- *How can I get that special someone interested in me?*
- *How do I make the right career choice?*
- *Is it healthy to go steady?*
- *How can I overcome my shyness and not be a wallflower?*
- *Should I go to college or get a job?*
- *How do I cope with other women in his life?*
- *How can I become better friends with my parents?*
- *What can I do about my differences with my parents on how to dress?*
- *If I plan to marry, is it worth the time and expense to get a college education?*
- *How can I get along better with my younger siblings?*
- *Is the popular teen-ager happy and well-adjusted?*
- *How do I introduce people properly and which fork should I use for each course?*

✎ 12-Year Old **Fred Safier, Jr**. Is Awarded Harvard Scholarship After Making A Perfect Mark In Advanced Mathematics In His College Entrance Examination.

✎ **Leonard Ross**, A 10-Year Old Student From California, Wins $100,000 Prize On A TV Quiz Show For Answering Correctly Questions On The Stock Market.

FOR A GUD TIEME, DOEN'T SPEL WEL

A study conducted at the University of California on the profile of a good speller revealed that women who are good spellers tend to be confident and possess social grace, while their male counterparts displayed the opposite qualities. It went on to say that the poor spellers from both sexes tended to be more relaxed about life in general, didn't need to be intellectual and were quite at ease in social situations.

THE COLLEGIATE WHEEL OF FORTUNE
THE EARNING STATISTICS

Average Tuition (Four Years): $9,000
Earnings Potential: $100,000 More Over A Lifetime Than A High School Graduate.
Exception: One-fourth of college graduates will earn less than the average holder of a high school diploma only.

SAVE $10

THIS PAGE IS WORTH $10
on this *new* dramatically styled
LANE CEDAR CHEST!

UNTIL MIDNIGHT FEB. 29

This exciting new Crestlane model is a... **$59**⁹⁵ VALUE

However, if you tear out this page and take it, before midnight February 29, to your dealer featuring this offer— you pay only... **$49**⁹⁵!*

$1 down, $1 weekly at most furniture and department stores.

The Crestlane

New, spacious ultra-modern chest in Seafoam Mahogany with brass pulls. Exclusive self-lifting tray. Also in Pearl Gray Mahogany, Cordovan Mahogany, Charcoal Mahogany or Blond Oak.

Yes, take this page, before midnight February 29, to your dealer featuring this introductory offer on Lane's magnificent new Crestlane designs! The page becomes a *$10 Savings Certificate* toward your purchase of either model.

And here's a tip to thrifty gift-givers . . . buy *now* during this fabulous February savings event and have the Lane Chest delivered later—for a birthday, an engagement, wedding, anniversary . . . and—what could be more logical—for graduation! Your Lane dealer will be very glad to reserve your chest, on an easy layaway plan, to insure delivery whenever you want it. But by all means, take this page to your dealer *immediately* and save the $10.00!

Lane is the ONLY pressure-tested, aroma-tight cedar chest. Made of ¾ inch red cedar in accordance with U. S. Government recommendations, with a free moth protection guarantee underwritten by one of the world's largest insurance companies, issued upon proper application. Helpful hints for storing are in each chest. The Lane Company, Inc., Dept. L, Altavista, Va. In Canada: Knechtels, Ltd., Hanover, Ont.

The Crestlane DeLuxe

Features large base drawer; in Pearl Gray Mahogany as shown; also in Seafoam Mahogany, Cordovan Mahogany, Charcoal Mahogany or Blond Oak. A **$69.95** value, your choice of finish, only **$59.95*** when you present this page to your dealer.

SAVE $10

A THRIFTY IDEA FOR A SUPERB VALENTINE ON FEB. 14th

Federation Of Jewish Philanthropies Presents Awards

Dinner guests gather at the Hotel Sheraton Astor for the third annual presentation of achievement awards by the Amusement Division of the Federation of Jewish Philanthropies.

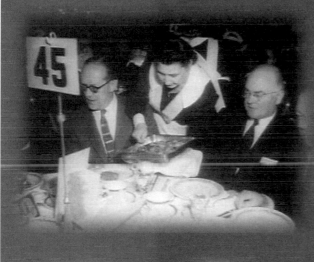

Steve Allen, star of "The Benny Goodman Story," presents an award to **Paul Muni.**

TOP MAGAZINES

Reader's Digest
Life
Saturday Evening Post
Look
Collier's
Ladies Home Journal
Better Homes and Gardens

Honorees **Kim Novak** and **Phil Silvers** kibitz with each other after receiving their awards.

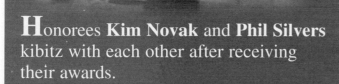

WHAT A YEAR IT WAS!

JUST A LITTLE SQUEEZE WILL DO YA

If you thought the proper way to judge cheese was by sniffing, well, think again. According to professional cheese testers, the correct procedure is to gently press the thumb into the cheese which allows them to evaluate its texture, body, firmness and oh yes, its flavor, too. Boy, this brie feels delicious!

- The Food & Drug Administration Rescinds Order Banning The Dying Of Oranges To Make Them Look More Appetizing.

- Heinz, Beech-nut, Brillo And Curtiss Candy Among National Brands Adding Kosher Products To Their Lines.

■ A Dramatic Increase In Navy Bad-Conduct Discharges Is Blamed On A Trend Toward Moral Decline And Irresponsibility Among Adolescents.

■ Insisting That A Child Be Overly Concerned With Neatness Can Stifle Artistic Development.

■ Unhappy Childhoods And Fear Of Failure Often Motivate Success Drive.

■ Psychological Treatment Found More Effective In Treating Female Homosexuals Than Their Male Counterparts.

Pyromaniacs Found To Be Raised In Homes With Indifferent Mothers And Abusive Fathers And Set Fires In A Misguided Effort To Find Their Manhood.

TO AVOID OVERLOADING YOUR MEMORY, WHEN YOU GO GROCERY SHOPPING MEMORIZE ONLY SEVEN ITEMS TO BUY, WHICH IS ABOUT THE NUMBER THE AVERAGE PERSON CAN CARRY IN HIS MIND AT ANY SINGLE TIME.

NEW SUBWAY IN LENINGRAD

Russia's second-largest city opens a new subway system with tunnels that fan out from the city center to serve outlying industrial areas.

The first train leaves the central station with a group of factory workers.

The opening is marked by ranking dignitaries from Moscow.

Scenes of Russian history are depicted in the ornate stations.

Kentucky Fried Chicken Begins Franchising.

Crest Toothpaste Is Distributed Nationally.
Pepsodent Introduces Its Catchy Jingle:
*"You'll Wonder Where The Yellow
Went When You Brush Your Teeth With Pepsodent."*

Navy Balloonists Soar To Record Altitude of 76,000 Ft.

Captain Midnight Decoder Ring Becomes Popular Fad.

Snow Falls On The Riviera As Severe Cold Wave Hits Europe.

THE FBI SOLVES THE BRINK'S ROBBERY AFTER A 5-YEAR INVESTIGATION—NO MONEY IS TRACED OR RECOVERED.

IRS Shuts Down Left-Wing Publication, DAILY WORKER, For Tax Evasion.

USS SARATOGA, World's Biggest Warship, Is Commissioned At Brooklyn Navy Yard.

President Eisenhower Creates Federal Council On Aging.

In A 5-To-4 Decision, The U.S. Supreme Court Holds That New York City Did Not Have The Right To Dismiss A Professor For Invoking The Protection Of The 5th Amendment.

U.S. Air Force Chief Of Staff, General Nathan F. Twining, Authorized By Ike To Accept Invitation To Attend Soviet Air Show.

Motorized Go-Carts Debut In Los Angeles.

YOUNGEST GOLFER TOURS COUNTRY TO RAISE FUNDS FOR THE BABE ZAHARIAS CANCER FUND

With the aplomb of a grown-up and the polish of a pro, 5-year old golf child prodigy, Linda Lewis, swings away at the Clearview Course on Long Island.

Linda's dad demonstrates his utmost confidence and lets her really get his teeth into one of her shots.

$10,000 A YEAR LIFESTYLE

- **Upper Stratum Of Community**
- **Comfortable House**
- **Nice Car**
- **Good Schools For Children**
- **Good Credit**

DAILY COST OF TRAVELLING TO WORK

By Car . . . . $.26
Bus Or Subway . . $.28

- The "Trip Finder"— A Group Of Sectional Highway Maps—Is Introduced As A Travel Aid.

- Hot-Rodders Turn Drag-Racing Into Sophisticated Sport.

- President Eisenhower Signs Historic Public Works Bill Authorizing Over $33 Billion For Nationwide Network Of Highways Linking Major American Cities.

Armies Of
Large Red Ants
Attack Traffic
Control Boxes
In Los Angeles
Causing Traffic
Signal
Failure.

President Eisenhower Authorizes FBI Intervention In Kidnapping Cases 24 Hours After Commission Of The Crime Instead Of The Former 7-Day Waiting Period.

Nobel Peace Prize Committee Announces It Could Not Find A Worthy Recipient For The 1956 Prize.

U.S. Government Announces It Will Help Transport Over 1,000 Afghan Moslems On Their Pilgrimage To Mecca.

The Life Expectancy Of A Child Born In 1956 Is 75 Years Of Age With An Annual Earning Potential Of $8,000 By The Year 2000.

Stop-Watch Tests Reveal That A Golfer Spends An Average 12 Minutes Of Actual Playing Time On An 18-Hole Course.

HERE'S THE DOPE ON DOPE	➠ The U.S. has more drug addicts than all other Western nations combined. ➠ Illegal drug traffic has tripled since World War II. ➠ Drug addicts commit an estimated 50% of urban crimes.

• President Eisenhower Approves Bill Authorizing Death Penalty For Selling Or Giving Heroin To Anyone Under 18.

According To A Report Released By A Group Of New York Psychoanalysts, Homosexual Men Played With Dolls Instead Of Playing Baseball As Youngsters.

PRESIDENT OF NICHOLS WIRE & ALUMINUM CO. BELIEVES A LOW-COST DISPOSABLE CAR WILL DOMINATE THE AMERICAN AUTO MARKET BY 1966.

Marriage Hits A Record High For American Men.

WHAT A YEAR IT WAS!

▶ **Advertisers Who Hook Children To Their Products Between The Ages Of 7 To 18 Are Apt To Have Lifetime Loyalty.**

▶ **Bizarre Food Cravings Linked To Possible Physical Deficiencies.**

▶ **Contentment With Life And Acceptance Of Its Realities Decreases Boredom In Workplace.**

 Trans-Atlantic Phone Service Begins, Linking Newfoundland to Scotland.

Buddhism's 2,500 Anniversary Celebrated In India.

WHAT'S A FEW YEARS AMONG FRIENDS?

After medical authorities in New York examined Colombian Indian, Javier Pereira, who claimed to be 167 years old, they admitted that he might be more than 150 years old.

THE SHORT END OF THE CHALK

Tokyo school officials defended their decision not to hire any teacher under 5 feet tall on the grounds that (a) it would be difficult to locate her during outdoor activities and (b) she would not be able to reach the blackboard.

• PASSINGS •

Jake "Greasy Thumb" Guzik, Associate Of Al Capone, Dies At 69.

Samuel James Seymour, Believed To Be Last Surviving Witness Of Lincoln's Assassination, Dies At 96.

Lewis Terman, Creator Of The IQ Test, Dies At 79.

Last Surviving Member Of The Civil War's Union Army, **Albert Woolson**, 109, Dies In Duluth, Minnesota.

BUSINESS

RCA Converts A Portion Of Its Black And White Television Production Lines To Color In Anticipation Of Increased Sales.

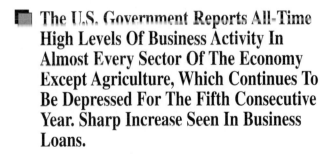

- The U.S. Government Reports All-Time High Levels Of Business Activity In Almost Every Sector Of The Economy Except Agriculture, Which Continues To Be Depressed For The Fifth Consecutive Year. Sharp Increase Seen In Business Loans.

- Thomas J. Watson Sr. (82) Retires As Chief Executive Officer Of IBM And Is Replaced By Son, Thomas, Jr.

- Missouri Pacific Railroad Restored To Private Ownership After Being In Bankruptcy Since 1933.

- Rockefeller Institute Announces Establishment Of Graduate School For Outstanding Scholars In Biology And Medicine.

SEPTEMBER

The Gross National Product Reaches All-Time High of $413,000,000,000.

- National Federation Of Business & Professional Women's Convention Adopts Resolution In Favor Of Equal Pay For Women And Men Doing Comparable Work.

- Government Announces Law Suit Against General Motors Under The Sherman Anti-Trust Act On Charges That GM Conspired With Four Bus Companies To Maintain A Monopoly.

this was the price that was

Billfold, ladies'	$ 5.00
Chest of drawers	99.50
China dinnerware (5 piece place setting)	11.95
Cookie sheet	1.15
Dining table	159.00
Measuring cup, glass	.79

Mixing bowls, set of 4	$ 2.95
Percolator, electric	19.95
Pie plate, glass	.59
Pressure cooker	29.95
Roasting pan	4.75

Saucepan	$ .65
Sewing pattern	.25
Sofa bed	259.50
Step stool	13.95
Sterling silver flatware (6 piece place setting)	33.50
Suitcase, ladies'	25.00
Tableware, service for 8	69.75
Teakettle	5.45
Vinyl flooring (8'x10')	21.50

House, Readi-cut

$1,985.00

WHAT A YEAR IT WAS!

Ladies'
• CLOTHING •

Designer Dress
$195.00 to $365.00

WHAT-NOT-STORE

ITEM	PRICE
Bra	$3.95
Girdle	8.95
Panties	0.89
TOTAL	**$13.79**

Thank You

La Shop

Coat	$50.00
Cotton dress	5.98
Playsuit w/skirt	14.98
Summer dress	14.95
Shoes, leather	8.95
Shoes, canvas	3.95

Average Yearly Driving Costs For A Family Of Four For 15,000 Miles

Depreciation	**$481.33**
Gasoline & Oil	**348.00**
Insurance	**104.39**
License Fees	**16.86**
Maintenance	**111.00**
Tires	**76.50**

MEN'S CLOTHING

Coat	∽	$59.50
Necktie	∽	2.50
Oxford shirt	∽	5.00
Wool slacks	∽	22.50
Wool suit	∽	65.00

LONG DISTANCE
TELEPHONE RATES*

San Francisco to Washington, D.C. . . .	$2.00
Milwaukee to New York	1.20
Dallas to Denver	1.10
Chicago to Buffalo	.95
New York to Boston	.55
Pittsburgh to Cleveland	.45

***First 3 minutes, evenings and Sundays**

WHAT A YEAR IT WAS!

81

Famous Swanson Pies now even better!

More meat—yes, more meat than you ever get in those so-called "bargain" pies.

Extra flaky crusts—that go the whole way around. No skimping here or anywhere.

Rare old-time goodness in the savory, rich gravy. Exceptional taste and flavor.

Compare the goodness of these wonderful Swanson Pies with any pie you've ever tasted – even your own! See the difference for yourself. You can do it now at a big 50¢ saving. See offer below!

Swanson is a trademark owned by the makers of Campbell's Soups.

The Ford Foundation Makes First Public Offering Of Its Stock.

American Telephone And Telegraph Company Announces Plans To Offer 5,750,000 Shares Of Common Stock To Its Shareholders, Making It The Largest Common Stock Offering In History.

U.S. Antitrust Suit Against American Telephone And Telegraph Settled By Consent Decree — Patents Open To All Applicants.

650,000 U.S. Steelworkers Strike.

Westinghouse Electric And International Union Of Electrical Workers Settle Longest Major Strike (156 Days) In 20 Years.

Federal Reserve Board And Federal Deposit Insurance Corp. Announce **3%** U.S. Commercial Banks Will Be Allowed To Pay A Maximum 3% Interest Rate On Savings Deposits Effective January 1, 1957.

ELECTRONICS U.S. FIFTH LARGEST INDUSTRY

U.S. Labor Secretary, James Mitchell, Reports U.S. Employment As Of August Was At An All-time High.

WHAT A YEAR IT WAS!

PASSINGS

THOMAS J. WATSON,
Chairman Of The Board Of IBM,
Dies At 82.

WILLIAM BOEING,
Pioneer In Aircraft Technology,
Dies At 74.

CLARENCE BIRDSEYE,
Inventor Of Quick Freezing
Process For Foods,
Dies At 69.

CHARLES EDWARD MERRILL,
Founder Of Merrill Lynch,
Started Safeway Stores And
Family Circle Magazine,
Dies At 70.

SAMUEL A. LERNER,
Founder Of Lerner Stores,
Dies At 72.

HARRY FORD SINCLAIR,
Founder Of Sinclair Oil Corp.,
Dies At 80.

MARSHALL FIELD III,
Heir To Chicago Store Millions,
Dies at 63.

Try Spiced Luncheon Meat, mustard relish, lettuce.

Try Hard Salami on soft bun with lettuce, onion.

Try tender Cooked Ham, Swiss cheese on rye.

Try Cooked Salami with mustard, dill slices, egg.

Try P & P Loaf on whole wheat with mayonnaise.

Try Bologna on Russian rye with egg salad.

Good meat _makes_ a sandwich! And you know it's FRESH when you see the Swift's Premium brand! More than 100 Swift's Premium Table-Ready Meats are made FRESH daily in nearby kitchens... rushed to your store. Every week _millions_ of packages are sold.

Swift's Premium Table Ready Meats are served exclusively in Disneyland, Anaheim, California

84

SCIENCE & MEDICINE

- ✦ **T**he Neutrino, Atomic Particle With No Electric Charge, Discovered At Los Alamos Laboratory In U.S.

- ✦ **I**on Microscope Developed by F.W. Muller.

- ✦ **N**uclear Reactor Opens In Harwell, England.

- ✦ **AEC** Approves Private Nuclear Reactor In Indian Point, N.Y.

- ✦ **A**tomic Expert Warns That Major Technical Obstacles Must Be Overcome In Order To Develop Practical, Low-Cost Nuclear Power.

- ■ Atlantic City Report Links Lung Cancer To Air Pollution.
- ■ U.S. Committee Of Scientists Reports That Exposure To Even The Smallest Amounts Of Atomic Radiation Harms Not Only The Recipient But Future Generations As Well.

NOBEL PRIZES

MEDICINE

Andre F. Cournand (U.S.)

Werner Forssman (Germany)

Dickinson W. Richards, Jr. (U.S.)

PHYSICS

John Bardeen, Walter H. Brattain, William Shockley (all U.S.)

CHEMISTRY

Sir Cyril N. Hinshelwood (Great Britain)

Nikolai N. Semenov (USSR)

Medicine

Salk Polio Vaccine Made Available To Public – Jonas Salk Predicts Elimination Of Polio By 1959.

FIRST PREFRONTAL LOBOTOMY PERFORMED AT GEORGE WASHINGTON UNIVERSITY.

DR. ALBERT SABIN

Develops Oral Polio Vaccine.

Israeli Scientists Develop Test To Determine Sex Of Fetus After Twelfth Week Of Pregnancy By Extracting Sample Of Amniotic Fluid.

Dr. Landrum B. Shettles Of Columbia University Develops Procedure For Determining The Sex Of An Unborn Baby Through Amniotic Fluid Extracted In The Ninth Month Of Pregnancy. Technique For Safe Extraction Still Being Worked On.

A Significant Relationship Is Found Between Physical And Mental Illnesses.

Mental Patients Account For More Hospital Beds Than All Other Patients Combined.

WHAT A YEAR IT WAS!

According To Dr. Nathan Millman Of The Ortho Research Foundation In New Jersey, There Is No Magic Birth Control Tablet Than Can Produce Temporary Sterility In A Patient.

Women Test First Birth Control Pill In Puerto Rico And Haiti.

Successful Pregnancy Rate Low For Women 44 Years Of Age Or Older According To Report Released By Dr. E.F. Stanton.

TEMPER, THY NAME BE WOMAN

A study conducted at a New York hospital confirmed what doctors already suspected – that hypertension with its resultant emotional, sometimes dramatic mood swings, is connected to underlying emotional disturbances. Some of their findings:

• More women than men suffer from hypertension;

• Unexpressed emotions are major contributing factors;

• Women's need to please prevents expression of emotions which, in addition to mood swings, can manifest in other disorders such as migraine headaches and other physical symptoms.

Unsure as to exactly how to treat this disorder, one doctor concluded that if the patient has no previous symptoms, the kindest thing he can do is to keep to the information to himself.

Yes Virginia, You Have Pre-Menstrual Blues

A study conducted by English husband and wife team, Drs. Iain and Pamela MacKinnon, presented medical evidence that in the few days preceding menstruation, women experience cellular changes causing them to be more prone to emotional Instability including increased capability of committing crimes of violence.

New wonder of nutrition found in the fresh orange

The BIO-FLAVONOIDS, mysterious yellow substances in the "meat" of the fruit, affect your family's health in a special way all their own

The list of health values in the fresh orange has continued to mount through the years... vitamin C, pro-vitamin A, B vitamins, minerals, amino acids, the remarkable protopectins.

Now the bio-flavonoids are making front-page news. Science knows now that the bio-flavonoids, when teamed with vitamin C in oranges, fortify body health from childhood to old age in a new way largely overlooked in the past.

They have a direct effect *on the capillary system* ... the millions of tiny blood vessels that nourish every part of your body. They help keep these tiny vessels strong and elastic... *efficient* in their job. They also strengthen weak capillaries. Thus, when combined with other factors in the fresh orange, they have an important bearing on the prevention of disease, the way your children grow, the way *you* look and feel!

One Sunkist Orange a day gives you a rich supply of bio-flavonoids. They are abundant in the *fresh* orange but not in processed juice. Like the recently announced protopectins, they are found almost entirely in the "meat" of the fresh orange. And they are scarce in most other foods.

Shouldn't you see that each member of your family eats one fresh orange every day?

◄◄ **Healthy children.** The bio-flavonoids team with vitamin C and many other values in fresh oranges to do a better job of building sturdy bones and strong muscles, developing sound teeth and gums, fighting colds and infections.

▲ **Your own good health.** The bio-flavonoids work with vitamin C in fresh oranges to keep your capillary system young, to give you extra energy and the glow of health.

Sunkist Navel Oranges are wonderful eating. Easy to peel, no seeds, richer flavor. How fortunate that this luscious fruit is so important to health. Look for the name Sunkist on the skin.

▲ **60,000 miles long!** Your capillary system would circle the earth 2½ times. It's little wonder doctors say, "You're only as young as your capillaries."

▲ **Nothing so easy to serve** as Sunkist Navel Oranges! *Just hand them out*—after school, after meals, at TV time. When you squeeze them for juice, don't strain it. Keep the healthful solids that contain the bio-flavonoids and so many other values.

Sunkist Growers *California-Arizona Navel Oranges*

Eat whole fresh oranges—drink whole fresh orange juice!

CANCER UP-DATE

According to a cancer report published in the A.M.A. Journal, despite an increase in life expectancy, research revealed the following grim statistics:

• 36 out of 100 females and 31 out of 100 males born this year will die of cancer.

• Reported cancer cases will increase by over 50% within the next 25 years.

• Cancer occurs at the same rate for men and women, but more men die because of the inaccessibility of the afflicted areas.

• More cases are reported in urban than rural areas while fewer cases are reported among non-whites than whites.

• Sloan-Kettering Institute announces breast cancer may be diagnosed through component found in the blood.

• New sulfur mustard drug appears promising in treatment of Hodgkin's Disease and other forms of lymphatic cancer according to scientists at University of California at San Francisco.

• Abnormal protein found in the blood of cancerous mice.

• The "Smear Technique" found useful in detection of skin cancer.

Doctors Report Link Between Cigarette Smoking And Pulmonary Emphysema.

Cancer Recovery Rate Rises To 50% As A Result Of Early Diagnosis, Surgery And Radiation Therapy.

Bill To Legalize Corneal Transplants Is Introduced In Italy After Successful, Illegal Operation Performed By Distinguished Surgeon, Dr. Cesare Galeazzi. Current Law Forbids Mutilation Of Corpses Within 24 Hours After Death.

A WONDERFUL NEW WAY TO CONTROL WEIGHT

NEW Pearson sakrin

The ONLY Liquid Sweetener with DARAMIN®, containing

NO Calories! NO Sugar! NO Salt!

Use it in coffee, tea, hot or cold beverages, mixed drinks, cereals, desserts, cooking!

It's *super-concentrated* — only 1 drop equals the sweetness of 1 whole teaspoon of sugar!

69¢ PEARSON SAKRIN equals sweetening power of **OVER 10 LBS. of SUGAR** SAVES YOU 18,144 CALORIES!

$1.49 PEARSON SAKRIN equals sweetening power of **OVER 25 LBS. of SUGAR** SAVES YOU 45,359 CALORIES!

NEW PEARSON LIQUID SAKRIN PUTS SWEETNESS IN, LEAVES CALORIES OUT — will help you be slim, stay slim, look better, feel better — every meal, every day. And you'll sacrifice *nothing* in flavor or enjoyment!

Excess weight is a threat to your health. Science shows that heart disease, high blood pressure and many other ills are more common in overweight persons. *Only 100 calories extra a day can put on ten extra pounds of fat a year!* PEARSON SAKRIN can help you avoid *hundreds* of extra calories a day.

EACH DROP SAVES CALORIES!

1 DROP equals 1 TSP. SUGAR

One tiny drop of PEARSON SAKRIN from its attractive squeezable dropper bottle — gives you the sweetening power of 1 teaspoon of sugar *without any of its calories!* In just coffee, tea, with desserts and in cooking, it can save you up to 511 calories and more a day — *that equals over one pound of weight a week* in "sweetening calories" alone!

Unlike some sweeteners that require you to use 2 to 5 drops per teaspoon of sugar, just 1 drop of PEARSON SAKRIN does the job. And it leaves no bitter after-taste.

So start with new PEARSON SAKRIN Liquid Sweetener today. Carry the regular container to use at lunch and coffee-breaks. Get the super size to keep at home on the table.

HOW PEARSON SAKRIN CAN SAVE YOU 511 CALORIES DAILY

(in foods where you usually use sugar)

		CALORIES ADDED BY:	
		PEARSON SAKRIN	SUGAR
Breakfast	Fruit Juice	0	16 (1 tsp.)*
	Cereal	0	32 (2 tsp.)
	Coffee or Tea	0	32 (2 tsp.)
Morning Break:	Coffee or Tea	0	32 (2 tsp.)
Lunch:	Fruit Cup	0	32 (2 tsp.)
	Dessert	0	32 (2 tsp.)
	Tea	0	32 (2 tsp.)
Afternoon Break:	Coffee or Tea	0	32 (2 tsp.)
Dinner:	Grapefruit	0	32 (2 tsp.)
	Dessert	0	32 (2 tsp.)
	Coffee or Tea	0	32 (2 tsp.)
Misc. sweetening, incl. mixed drinks, snacks while watching TV, as well as between meals and late evening snacks, etc.		0	175
TOTAL DAILY CALORIES SAVED WITH PEARSON SAKRIN			511

*LEVEL TEASPOON

Figure out your daily calorie savings with PEARSON SAKRIN — there may be more or less than above — but every calorie you save helps control weight! **SAVE ONE POUND A WEEK IN SWEETENING CALORIES ALONE!**

SAVES YOU MONEY, TOO!

MAKE THIS TASTE TEST!

Try coffee sweetened with sugar, and coffee sweetened with PEARSON SAKRIN. You can't tell the difference — PEARSON SAKRIN SAVES YOU MANY CALORIES EACH CUP!

GOOD HOUSEKEEPING GUARANTY SEAL!

The world-famous Good Housekeeping Laboratory has studied PEARSON SAKRIN thoroughly and finds it completely effective in providing sweetening with NO Calories, NO Sugar, NO Salt (sodium-free). Therefore PEARSON SAKRIN has earned the Good Housekeeping Seal as a most valuable aid in weight control, reducing diets, other cases, saving hundreds of calories daily.

Guaranteed by Good Housekeeping

REGULAR SIZE — 69¢
(Equals sweetness of over 10 lbs. Sugar)

SUPER SIZE — $1.49
(Equals sweetness of over 25 lbs. Sugar)

SAVES YOU CALORIES — SAVES YOU MONEY, TOO!

Free

...In every package of PEARSON SAKRIN — helpful reducing guide: "PEARSON SAKRIN WAY TO SLIMNESS".

PEARSON PHARMACAL CO., INC.
LONG ISLAND CITY, N. Y.

Get PEARSON SAKRIN now at Drug Stores, Supermarkets, Grocers, Dept. Stores

Pearson sakrin

LIQUID SWEETENER with exclusive DARAMIN

A national research council set up by the U.S. Food & Drug Administration concluded that poisoning or cancer could result from ingesting of dyes used in coloring food, lipstick and medicines. The report indicated that with its current staffing, it would take the FDA approximately 25 years to test the 116 dyes now certified as harmless.

A High-Salt Diet Is Linked To High Blood Pressure

This Could Drive You To Drink

The Alcoholic Personality Is A Result Of Drinking And Not The Original Cause Of Drinking According to Dr. Robert Fleming, Director Of The Alcoholism Clinic At Boston's Peter Bent Brigham Hospital.

On The Other Hand...

Dr. Giorgio Lolli, Director Of Silkworth Memorial Service At New York's Knickerbocker Hospital, Believes In A Pre-Alcoholic And Alcoholic Personality With Heredity And Environmental Influences Acting As Contributing Factors.

1956

Medicine

The American Psychiatric Association issued a warning to its members against the use of tranquilizers as medicine for the relief of everyday tensions and that casual use of such drugs was considered medically unsound and a public danger.

A Brain Storm

British Neurologist, Sir Russell Brain, Applauds Charles Dickens For His Impressive Medical Accuracy In Describing The Variety Of Diseases He Inflicted On His Characters.

With the rise in diabetes among children, the University of Rochester published its observations as follows:

1 Being underweight, not overweight plays a major role;

2 Eating sweets is not a causal factor;

3 Insulin treatment is necessary in most cases;

4 Flexibility should be practiced for special occasions such as birthday celebrations so that the child does not feel deprived.

New Findings Suggest That Booster Polio Shots May Not Be Necessary After Initial Immunization By Salk Vaccine.

Saliva May Play Important Role In Preventing Tooth Decay According To Dr. C.E. Krapper Of The University Of Alabama Medical Center.

WHAT A YEAR IT WAS!

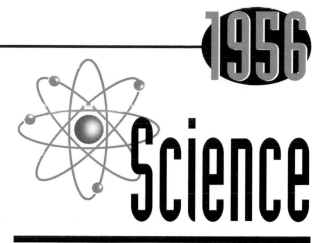

1956

Science

- Scientists Report Surface Of Venus Too Hot To Support Life As We Know It.

- Earth's First Man-Made Satellite Nears End Of Planning Stage.

- Cosmic Rays Bombard Earth At Phenomenal Rate Indicating Cosmic Rays Can Originate In The Solar System As Well As Outer Space.

Radiation Victims Who Do Not Vomit Immediately After Exposure Have Higher Rate Of Survival Than Those Who Vomit Immediately After Being Exposed.

First Films Of Ground-To-Air Guided Missiles In Action Released By Great Britain.

The U.S. Army Buys Experimental Models Of An Aerocycle, A One-Man Flying Machine Designed To Give The Infantryman More Mobility.

WITHOUT A *twist* PLEASE

A post-war orthopedic disorder has developed in Great Britain called "espresso wrist" as a result of twisting the hand during the preparation of demitasse. The cure: hold the wrist straight.

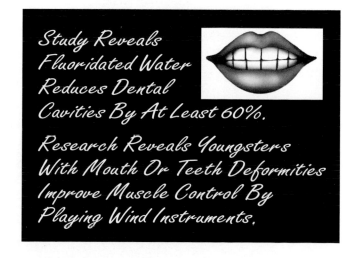

Study Reveals Fluoridated Water Reduces Dental Cavities By At Least 60%.

Research Reveals Youngsters With Mouth Or Teeth Deformities Improve Muscle Control By Playing Wind Instruments.

MONSANTO CHEMISTRY IN ACTION . . . COMMUNICATIONS

BUSY AMERICANS ENJOY THE EXTRA STYLE, COMFORT AND CONVENIENCE THAT MONSANTO CHEMICALS ADD *(left to right)* TO TELEPHONES—GLARE-

MONSANTO TAPS CHEMISTRY TO

Mixing creative research with production know-how, Monsanto tailors myriads of

NEW HEARING AID HIDES behind your ear, takes up only one cubic inch of space, operates with a flick of your finger. The tiny transmitter—including case made of Monsanto plastic—weighs less than an ounce. In a few minutes, you forget you have it on! Simple one-piece construction makes sound reception more natural than ever before, eliminates cords and bulky attachments.

DON'T BLAME YOUR PEN! Fuzzy writing (above, left) is no problem with stationery that has been treated with Monsanto chemicals. This fine paper (right) takes *and holds* a sharp ink line. Other Monsanto products lower the cost of making paper, help produce clearer blueprints . . . brighter paper . . . blacker inks with more body. Monsanto chemicals also help to mask printing ink odor.

REDUCING TV PICTURE FRAMES AND GLASS—LIGHT, COLORFUL RADIO CABINETS—UNBREAKABLE RECORDS—EASY-TO-READ BOOKS AND NEWSPAPERS

SERVE A LOOKING, LISTENING U. S.

products to meet the needs of people. Here are a few examples in Communications

POLES AND PEOPLE share the benefits of Penta, the *clean* wood preservative. Penta-treated poles resist rot and insects, last 30 years, won't stain hands or clothing.

HOUSEHOLD "HEAVYWEIGHT," the dependable telephone requires light, shock-absorbing parts. Monsanto makes tough plastics for the ear cap, mouthpiece and plugs ... vinyl wire-coatings that resist heat, cracks and age, come in different colors to make wires easy to identify.

MONSANTO

WHERE CREATIVE CHEMISTRY WORKS WONDERS FOR YOU

MANUFACTURERS: If you are interested in any of the above materials—are considering ways to use them in your business—or want more information, write Industrial Service Dept., Monsanto Chemical Company, St. Louis 4, Missouri. NEXT MONTH: MONSANTO CHEMISTRY IN RECREATION.

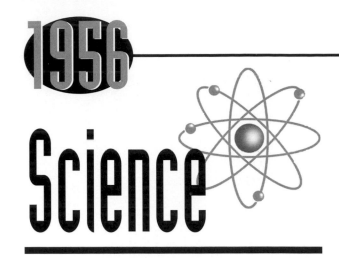

Science

Nobel Prize Winning Scientist Sir George Thomson Of Cambridge, England Predicts Monkeys Will Be Trained To Perform Certain Types Of Routine Work.

Scientists Predict Global Warming Trend For The Next 100 Years.

What do you mean, it won't fly?

Australian astronomer Richard van der Riet Woolley shook up the world of space research, declaring that no one will ever put up enough money to fund space travel. Leonard Carter of the British Interplanetary Society promptly declared that the first flight to the moon will take place in the next twenty years. Indignant Interplanetary Society Council member Kenneth Gatland added his opinion that space travel is inevitable and that toward the end of the century manned vehicles will orbit the moon with actual landings.

PASSINGS

Alfred Kinsey,
American Sexologist And Co-Author Of The Book, "Sexual Behavior In The Human Male", Dies At 62.

Dr. Hans S. Joachim,
Ex-Aide To Einstein, Developer Of Sound-Guided Torpedo, Dies At 68.

Cesare Barbieri,
Inventor Of Auto Antifreeze And Machines To Make Paper Cups, Dies At 78.

1956

INVENTIONS
Look, It's A Bird, It's A Plane, No . . . It's Supertrain

The air conditioned coach train, modern and streamlined, built by an auto maker carries 400 passengers.

The new, speedy, low center of gravity train promises fast, comfortable and less expensive rail travel.

The engineer settles in for the ride as the train is pulled swiftly and smoothly by its high powered diesel locomotive.

WHAT A YEAR IT WAS!

1956

New Heat Protective Suit Passes Furnace Test

In New York, engineer D.J. Bennett prepares to enter an industrial furnace to demonstrate a new heat protecting fabric lighter and more flexible than a fireman's rubber slicker.

The fabric is a micro-thin layer of reflective aluminum bonded to a backing of asbestos or fiberglass and is unmatched in its resistance to intense radiant heat.

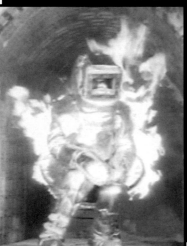

"The Grasshopper"

"The Grasshopper" is a robot weather station being tested at the Naval Research Laboratory for use in the Antarctic.

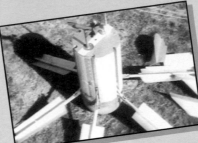

Looking more like a space creature, it stands up, raises its own antenna and other devices for weather recording.

The battery-powered robot transmits via radio data on wind speeds, temperature, pressure, etc., its signals being picked up 800 miles away.

HE FLIES THROUGH THE AIR WITH THE GREATEST OF EASE

This combination helicopter and boat sails through the air, borrowing its get up and go from an outboard tow boat.

inventions

- *Bell Telephone Begins "Visual Phone" Development.*

- *Largest Telescope In U.S. Unveiled At Harvard.*

- *Bette Nesmith Invents Liquid Paper.*

• Vending Machines Offering Full-Course Hot Meals For $.75 Begin To Replace Factory Cafeterias.

• Royal Typewriter Introduces New Typewriter Ribbon In Two Plastic Containers Allowing User To Change Ribbons Without Soiling Her Hands.

• *Microimage Device Gives Automatic Access To Up To 10,000 Microfilm Frames*

• Heated Flexible Windshield Glass To Protect Pilots From Collisions With Birds Is Developed By Pittsburgh Plate Glass Co.

• Hughes Aircraft Company Develops New Picture Tube With Stop-Action Capabilities For Air-Borne Radar.

¥ Color Television Programs Can Now Be Recorded On Ampex Magnetic Tape With Up To 15 Minutes Of Programming For Rebroadcast.

• *Hand-Held TV Camera Developed For The U.S. Army.*

DISCOVERIES • • • DISCOVERIES • • • DISCOVERIES

MuTaTiOn

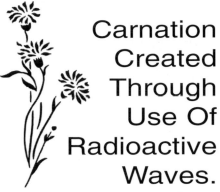

Carnation Created Through Use Of Radioactive Waves.

The Army Map Service Reports Earth 420 Feet Smaller Than Has Been Thought.

University Of California

Announces The Discovery Of The Antineutron, A New And Previously Unknown Particle, With The Property Of Destroying Matter In Its Ordinary State.

While you wash and dry the babies...

the fabulous Bendix Duomatic washes <u>and</u> <u>dries</u> their clothes!

In just <u>58</u> minutes their grimy play clothes can be <u>clean</u> and <u>dry</u>!

And half the time you'll *dress* your toddlers out of the Bendix Duomatic, too.

Simply turn the dial and the Duomatic takes over both the washing *and* drying ... does everything but fold the clothes.

All in one continuous, automatic operation! Without even a glance from you!

Here's the way it works

First ... the Duomatic washes and triple-rinses the famous Bendix Tumble-Action way. Then it automatically turns into a dryer that fluffs and tumbles the clothes completely, beautifully dry. And dressing the children out of the Duomatic is no dream. It's practical as can be. You can pop their things in the Duomatic any old time

... take them out ready for wearing. Cuts way down on the number of clothes they'll need.

If you want to "just wash"... or "just dry"

That's fine with the Duomatic! You can use it for washing only ... or drying only ... whenever you like. Just a touch of the dial and this wonderworker will do any washday chore you ask of it. Except, as we said before, fold the clothes!

Two models—gas or electric

Only Bendix gives you this choice ... and what a boon it is. You save all along the line with a machine that uses the fuel you prefer for your other appliances. And either one fits neatly into

just 36 inches of wall space. Price? You'll be happily surprised. As little as $3.20 a week!*

The advantages of Bendix Tumble-Action in a separate washer, too

If you already have a dryer, you can't have a better companion for it than the new 1956 Bendix Tumble-Action Washer...with all the special washing features developed for the Duomatic.

*After Minimum Down Payment

For the name of your nearest Bendix dealer, call Western Union Operator 25.

The new way of washing and drying you will surely come to...

BENDIX DUOMATIC
WASHER-DRYER ALL-IN-ONE

Crosley and Bendix Home Appliances Divisions of AVCO MANUFACTURING CORPORATION advanced development in Aviation, Electronics, Products for Farm and Home
In Canada, Crosley and Bendix Home Appliances are manufactured and distributed by Moffats Limited, Weston, Ontario

Now! Freezer Refrigerator Combinations designed specially for Supermarket Shoppers

Do you have room for the garden-fresh things now rushed to your store in and out of season? The bottles, baked goods, Supermarket Specials? You *will* have ... with the abundant storage space that only a Crosley "Fresh and Frozen Food Center" provides.

Today you're buying twice the frozen vegetables, ten times as many frozen meats as you did a few years ago. Your present refrigerator just wasn't built for this easy new era. But Crosley "Fresh and Frozen Food Centers" are ... with room for months of frozen fare!

The new way of food-keeping you will surely come to

Crosley "Fresh and Frozen Food Centers"

CROSLEY DUO-SHELVADOR
Refrigerator-Freezer All-in-One

A 13 cubic foot "Fresh and Frozen Food Center" in a single unit. Up top, a big 9.1 cubic foot refrigerator, with a 130 pound roll-out freezer below. Plus that deep, deep door, and the unique Crosley Beverage Server that serves ice water right through the door. Refrigerator *and* freezer defrost automatically in minutes, thanks to Crosley's new Hi-Speed Automatic Defrost. So fast, frozen foods stay frozen, never lose their vitamins or flavor.

Available in Color-Glo Yellow, Pink, Green, as well as White.

CROSLEY SHELVADOR TWINS
practically put the supermarket in your kitchen!

These two separate go-together units are the absolute ultimate in refrigeration. The "ALL" Refrigerator is ALL for fresh foods ... all 14 cubic feet of it. Because there is no freezer chest, you have 3½ extra bushels of room. And more in the Shelvador door, complete with the Beverage Server.

The matching Twin, Crosley's Shelvador Freezer, is all for frozen foods. Keeps 470 pounds within easy sight and reach. Use these Shelvador Twins side-by-side or separately. Each is only 31½ inches wide.

For the name of your nearest Crosley Dealer, call Western Union, Operator 25

CROSLEY

Crosley and Bendix Home Appliances Divisions of AVCO MANUFACTURING CORPORATION   advanced development in Aviation, Electronics, Products for Farm and Home
In Canada, Crosley and Bendix Home Appliances are manufactured and distributed by Moffats Limited, Weston, Ontario

1956

inventions

- Kodak Introduces Kodacolor Film Which Enables The Photographer To Use The Same Film For Indoor Or Outdoor Shots.

- General Motors Introduces Ultrasonic Dishwasher Which Uses Sound Waves To Remove Dirt As Part Of Its "Kitchen Of Tomorrow."

- Leroy Crozier Of Cincinnati, Ohio Invents A Portable Ironing Board.

- Fluoride Toothpaste Produces A 42% Reduction In Tooth Decay When Tested On 300 College Freshmen.

General Electric And The Westinghouse Electric Corp. Introduce Colored Light Bulbs For The Home.

TINY HOME FIRE ALARM DEVELOPED BY LARAMIE CHEMICAL CORP. OF STAMFORD, CONNECTICUT.

Central Air Conditioning System Introduced By Amana Refrigeration, Inc.

British Inventor Develops First Solar Energy House.

ZENITH RADIO CORP. INTRODUCES "SPACE COMMAND TV"– A REMOTE TUNER THAT CONTROLS THE TV SET.

Rubber Scrubber Corp., Watertown, New York, Invents New Household Scouring Device With Foam Rubber On One Side And An Abrasive Material On The Other.

New Process – "Instantizing"– Is Developed For Mixing Dried Foods.

Bell & Howell Introduces Automatic Movie Camera Which Sets The Lens At The Proper Exposure.

Aerosol Spray-On Shoe Polish Developed By Power-Matic Corp.

Johnson & Johnson Introduces A Non-Slip Cotton-Gauze Roller Bandage.

WHAT A YEAR IT WAS!

Long-life Stainless Steel Razor Blades Introduced By British Company, Wilkinson Sword.

Giant Forging Press, Largest Machine In The World, Goes Into Full Operation In North Grafton, Massachusetts.

New Packaging And Scanning Machinery Moves Production Line Consumer Goods Faster And Diminishes Mislabelling Possibilities.

The Mechanics And Farmers Savings Bank in Bridgeport, Connecticut, Introduces A Two-Way Screen And Speaker Set-Up Allowing The Customer To Communicate With The Teller Without Ever Leaving His Car.

Aerosol Containers Revolutionize The Cosmetic Industry.

Jet Propulsion Engines Debut And Go Into Production.

NEW CAR SAFETY DEVICES

▶ Latches that reduce the likelihood of doors flying open in crashes;

▶ Padding on instrument panels and visors;

▶ Seat belts

Liquefied Gas Produced On An Industrial Scale.

ELECTRONIC DEVICES OF THE FUTURE

- Equipment to heat or cool a room silently by electronic panels.
- A magnetic tape player that reproduces television programs using standard television receivers.
- An electronic light amplifier that increases up to 1,000 times the brightness of a projected image, including X-ray images of stationary objects.

"**THANK YOU THESE STAMPS ARE SANITARY**" The U.S. Post Office has introduced 'The Stampmaster', an automatic stamp dispenser which not only makes change and delivers stamps, but even has a built-in speaker to thank the customer and reassure her that the stamps are sanitary as well as a reminder to think about buying more now to save another trip to the post office.

NOW...HOT BEVERAGES *and* ICE CUBES...

with this New Hot 'n Cold Water Cooler!

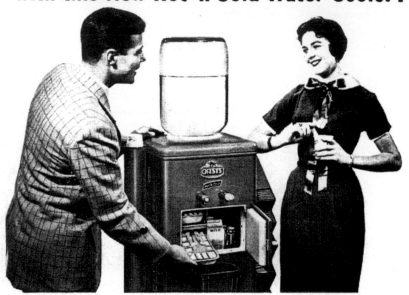

Think of it—a single water cooler that gives all three! Piping hot water for instant beverages. Delightfully cold water for drinking—*and now!* Two full trays of ice cubes in a roomy, refrigerated compartment that's big enough to keep bottled drinks, packed lunches, or *practically anything*—cold and safe!

Controls the Coffee-Break! Today thousands of office and factory workers enjoy a muss-free, fuss-free coffee-break *on the spot* with a new Oasis Hot 'n Cold. Serving piping hot water for instant beverages, the Hot 'n Cold is the quickest, most economical way of controlling the coffee-

break. There's no more going out or sending out for coffee. Actual case histories prove you can save thousands of dollars a year in lost time.

Here's more news! Now you can get freshly sealed, self-service envelopes of instant coffee; chocolate; beef, vegetable and chicken broth; Pream; sugar; cups; spoons and other supplies from your Oasis distributor or direct from Ebco.

Mail Coupon for the Facts . . . Let us send you documented evidence that the Hot 'n Cold is saving big money for users and prove what it can do for you. Learn about the new models.

Oasis HOT 'N COLD WATER COOLER

made in pressure and bottle models
"The Most Complete Line of Water Coolers"

THE EBCO MANUFACTURING COMPANY
Department SS, Columbus 13, Ohio

Send complete Hot 'n Cold information to:

name_____ title_____

company_____

address_____

city_____ zone_____ state_____

Model 13P-HC

DISTRIBUTED IN CANADA BY G. H. WOOD & CO., LTD.

ENTERTAINMENT

MOVIES

OSCAR NIGHT IN HOLLYWOOD

F ans gather outside the Pantages Theatre hoping to catch a glimpse of their favorite stars.

The star-studded crowd includes past Oscar winner Frank Sinatra and Jimmy Cagney, a contender for this year's Best Actor award.

Ernest Borgnine, congratulated by host Jerry Lewis, is named Best Actor of the year for his performance in "Marty" and receives his award from Grace Kelly.

Jerry Lewis presents the Oscar for Best Actress to Italian star Anna Magnani for her role in "The Rose Tattoo."

Marisa Pavan accepts on her behalf.

MOVIES

1956 Favorites
(Oscars Presented In 1957)

BEST PICTURE
Around The World In 80 Days

BEST ACTOR
YUL BRYNNER, *The King And I*

BEST ACTRESS
INGRID BERGMAN, *Anastasia*

BEST DIRECTOR
GEORGE STEVENS, *Giant*

BEST SUPPORTING ACTOR
ANTHONY QUINN, *Lust For Life*

BEST SUPPORTING ACTRESS
DOROTHY MALONE, *Written On The Wind*

BEST SONG
"Whatever Will Be, Will Be" (Qué Será, Será)

The Oscar Awards For 1955: Ceremony Held On March 21, 1956 And The Winner Is…

BEST PICTURE
Marty

BEST ACTOR
ERNEST BORGNINE, *Marty*

BEST ACTRESS
ANNA MAGNANI, *The Rose Tattoo*

BEST DIRECTOR
DELBERT MANN, *Marty*

BEST SUPPORTING ACTOR
JACK LEMMON, *Mr. Roberts*

BEST SUPPORTING ACTRESS
JO VAN FLEET, *East Of Eden*

BEST SONG
"Love Is A Many-Splendored Thing"

THE "CAMEO" APPEARANCE DEBUTS IN MIKE TODD'S "AROUND THE WORLD IN 80 DAYS".

1956 ADVERTISEMENT

Let Doris and Roy Pinney, famous husband-wife photographer team, help you choose

The Right Ansco
for Father, Mother, Daughter, Son

If he has a feeling for fine cameras—
precision-built 35mm camera at a popular price! Superb *f* 3.5 lens; action shutter (to 1/300). Lens-coupled range-view finder. Thumb-lever film transport. **Super Memar *f* 3.5, $69.50**

For a true hobbyist—first camera in America to feature new Light Value System, which many say is the photographic system of the future. *f*/3.5 lens; shutter speeds to 1/500; coupled rangefinder. 35mm. **Super Regent, $89.50**

If he has outgrown all but the best—newest 35mm camera in America, one of the finest ever to carry Ansco name, priced far lower than you'd expect! *f* 2 lens. Speeds to 1/500. Coupled rangefinder. **Super Memar *f* 2, $119.50**

"**Looks very slick indeed,**" says Doris, picking up an Anscoflex II. "A woman really would like this. Your subject shows up so clearly in the big viewing window. You can see what you're getting. No guesswork.

'Because a woman is home, she's able to take pictures on important occasions like birthdays. She's there and able to watch. So every woman should have a camera she can operate quickly and easily. It *is* quick and easy with this fixed-focus camera; you don't have to be a mechanical whiz to work it.

'The same reasons that make this a good camera for a woman, make it a fine choice for boys and girls, or for any beginner. The other fixed-focus camera, the Readyflash, is very easy to use, too—and a good size for taking with you."

With a man in mind, Roy Pinney points out that "The 35mm camera is becoming increasingly a color camera." He adds, "The more seriously a man regards color photography, the more you are justified in giving him the very finest 35mm camera Ansco makes.

"You'll notice they all have fine fast lenses and shutters, and many up-to-date features that help a man get better pictures. But even the simpler, less costly models are quite capable and take really fine color pictures."

The camera that understands a beginner...
and vice versa—Anscoflex II with big viewing window, built-in close-up lens and cloud filter. Plus leather case, flash unit and bulbs, film, travel kit. Worth $33.75. **Anscoflex II Outfit complete, $27.95**
Anscoflex I Outfit, $22.95

For a youngster—for anyone who wants pictures the easy way—Readyflash is the ready-set, all-fun, no-fuss camera! Plus flash unit and bulbs, Ansco film...all in handy travel kit. Worth $15.80. **Readyflash Outfit complete, $11.95**
Readyflash camera alone, $6.95

If he's ready to graduate to color pictures—
the 35mm Memar with color-corrected *f* 3.5 lens—plus leather case, flash unit, color film...all in a handsome travel kit. Worth $61.20. **Memar Outfit complete, $56.25**
Memar camera alone, $39.50

Wonderful "Stocking Gift"
... or when you want to make it a remembrance more substantial than a greeting card... a roll or two of Ansco All-Weather Pan black-and-white film. Or better still, Anscochrome color film!

Ansco 620
Ansco
NEW ALL-WEATHER PAN FILM

"Great Year" Camera

Christmas morning . . . as only Anscochrome can picture it!

Only with 3-times-faster Anscochrome . . .
Color pictures so charmingly true-to-life

Christmas is red and green, gold and silver. Christmas is a tree
and a feast and the family come together.
Christmas is the time of times for the great *new* color pictures you get with
Anscochrome . . . the super-speed successor to traditional color films.
Three-times-faster Anscochrome pictures Christmas in its true colors . . . the warm,
vibrant colors of life itself.   *Ansco, A Division of General Aniline & Film Corp., Binghamton, N. Y.*

**The super-speed successor to
traditional color film**
. . . available in 35mm, 120, 620, 828,
16mm movie and sheet sizes.

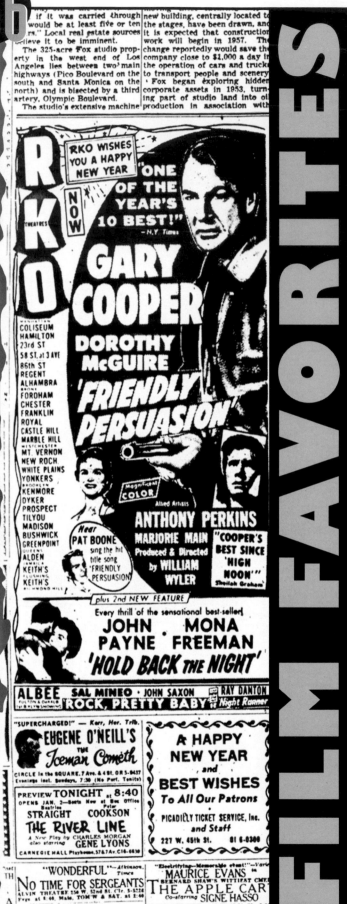

FILM FAVORITES

Alexander The Great

Anastasia

Anything Goes

Around The World In 80 Days

Baby Doll

Bigger Than Life

BUS STOP

CAROUSEL

Diane

FORBIDDEN PLANET

Forever Darling

Friendly Persuasion

Gaby

GIANT

Hell On Frisco Bay

High Society

I'll Cry Tomorrow

IT'S A **dOg's** LIFE

Lease Of Life

Lust For Life

Meet Me In Las Vegas

MOBY DICK

Picnic

Richard III

Romeo And Juliet

Somebody Up There Likes Me

Teahouse Of The August Moon

The Benny Goodman Story

The Bottom Of The Bottle

The Court Jester

The Harder They Fall

The Indian Fighter

The Invasion Of The Body Snatchers

THE KING AND I

The Ladykillers

The Last Wagon

The Littlest Outlaw

The Man In The Gray Flannel Suit

The Man Who Never Was

The Naked Sea

The Opposite Sex

THE RAINMAKER

The Searchers

THE SEVENTH SEAL

THE SOLID GOLD CADILLAC

THE TEN COMMANDMENTS

Too Bad She's Bad

War And Peace

WRITTEN ON THE WIND

You Can't Run Away From It

Rita Hayworth
Settles Nine-Month Feud
With Columbia Pictures.

BRIGITTE BARDOT BECOMES NEW FRENCH SEX KITTEN.

Boycott Of Non-Union Film "Daniel Boone" Demanded By A.F.L. Film Union.

Revised MPAA Censorship Code Discourages Racial Slurs And The Glorification Of Crime.

The Motion Picture Industry Revises And Relaxes Its Moral Code For The First Time Since Its Creation In 1930.

1956

TOP STARS

William Holden
John Wayne
James Stewart
Burt Lancaster
Glenn Ford
Dean Martin
   & Jerry Lewis
Gary Cooper
Marilyn Monroe
Kim Novak
Frank Sinatra
Lauren Bacall
Marlon Brando
Kirk Douglas
Henry Fonda
Cary Grant
Audrey Hepburn
Danny Kaye
Robert Taylor

STARS OF TOMORROW

Pier Angeli
Tony Curtis
Diana Dors
Anita Ekberg
Rock Hudson
Tab Hunter
Shirley Jones

Janet Leigh
Jack Lemmon
Gina Lollobrigida
Vera Miles
Aldo Ray
Yul Brynner
Joan Collins

Jeffrey Hunter
Sal Mineo
George Nader
Sheree North
Rod Steiger
Natalie Wood
Dana Wynter

FAMOUS BIRTHS

Lisa Hartman Black • Debby Boone • Delta Burke
David Copperfield • Bo Derek • Carrie Fisher
Andy Garcia • Mel Gibson • Tom Hanks
La Toya Jackson • Judge Reinhold • Eric Roberts
Bob Saget • Paula Zahn

Yul Brynner Brings
"The King & I"
To Hollywood After
Over 1,200 Broadway
Performances.

PASSINGS

ALEXANDER GILLESPIE RAYMOND, cartoonist, creator of "Flash Gordon", dies at 46.

CLARENCE E. MULFORD, creator of Hopalong Cassidy, dies at 73.

JACK COHN, co-founder of Columbia Pictures, dies at 67.

Danish-born actor, JEAN HERSHOLT, dies at 69 after a career spanning 50 years as a film star.

112

music

TOP 10 RECORDS

1. **Don't Be Cruel**
   Elvis Presley

2. **Great Pretender**
   The Platters

3. **My Prayer**
   The Platters

4. **Wayward Wind**
   Gogi Grant

5. **Whatever Will Be, Will Be (Qué Será Será)**
   Doris Day

6. **Heartbreak Hotel**
   Elvis Presley

7. **Lisbon Antigua**
   Nelson Riddle

8. **Canadian Sunset**
   Hugo Winterhalter

9. **Moonglow and Theme From "Picnic"**
   Morris Stoloff

10. **Honky Tonk**
    Bill Doggett

The Hits

Blueberry Hill

Blue Suede Shoes

Chain Gang

Flying Saucer (Parts I & II)

Green Door

Hot Diggity/Jukebox Baby

Hound Dog

I Almost Lost My Mind

I'm In Love Again

I Want You, I Need You, I Love You

Just Walking In The Rain

Long Tall Sally

Love Me Tender

Memories Are Made Of This

More

No, Not Much

Poor People Of Paris

Rock And Roll Waltz

Roll Over Beethoven

Singing The Blues

Standing On The Corner

The King Of Swing Swings With The King

Thailand's King Phumiphol Aduldet teams up with Benny Goodman for an impromptu jazz session.

WHAT A YEAR IT WAS!

 **1956**

ELVIS PRESLEY

Gains In Popularity And Makes His First Television Appearance Introduced By Tommy And Jimmy Dorsey.

A Record TV Audience Of An Estimated 54 Million People Tunes In To Watch Elvis Sing "Hound Dog" And "Love Me Tender" On The Ed Sullivan Show.

"Rock And Roll" Dance Becomes Popular.

NAT KING COLE ATTACKED DURING CONCERT IN BIRMINGHAM, ALABAMA.

Rock 'N' Roll
Revolutionizes The Recording Industry, Catapulting Black Artists Onto The Charts.

Bill Haley & His Comets Lose Favor With The Younger Audiences.

Annie Mae Bullock, 16, Changes Her Name To Tina Turner On Joining Ike Turner's Band.

Frankie Lymon Is Rock 'N' Roll's First Teenage Star At Age 13.

LIONEL HAMPTON DAZZLES FRENCH AUDIENCE IN JAZZ CONCERT.

RECORDING STARS OF TOMORROW

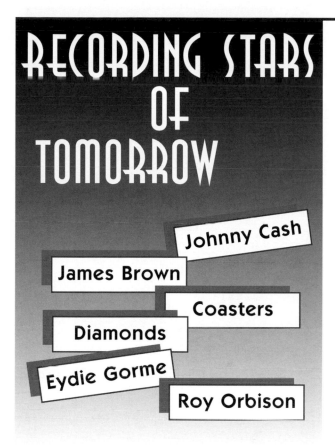

Johnny Cash

James Brown

Coasters

Diamonds

Eydie Gorme

Roy Orbison

TOP NETWORK RADIO PROGRAMS
SUMMER 1956

- ✧ **Best Of Groucho**
- ✧ **Truth Or Consequences**
- ✧ **Godfrey's Talent Scouts**
- ✧ **Hambletonian Stakes**
- ✧ **News From NBC**
- ✧ **Gangbusters**
- ✧ **Treasury Agent**
- ✧ **True Detective Mysteries**

OTHER RADIO FAVORITES

Aunt Jenny	Helen Trent
House Party	My True Story
Nora Drake	Our Gal Sunday
Road Of Life	Second Mrs. Burton

Young Dr. Malone

FRED ALLEN, radio entertainer whose radio program "Allen's Alley" drew an estimated 20 million listeners, dies at 61 of a heart attack.

PASSINGS

TOMMY DORSEY, "Sentimental Gentleman of Swing", dies at 51, leaving the legacy of "the greatest all-around dance band of them all." Frank Sinatra, vocalist for the band in the 40's, credited his vocal phrasing to Mr. Dorsey's extraordinary trombone musicianship.

ART TATUM, American jazz pianist, dies at 46.

DANNY RUSSO, composer of "Toot, Toot, Tootsie Goodbye", 71.

ALBERT VON TILZER, composer of "Take Me Out To The Ball Game", "I'll Be With You In Apple Blossom Time", 78.

ISHAM JONES, composer of "It Had To Be You", "I'll See You In My Dreams", 63.

RADIO

television

Get Out Your Hankies Ladies

The first soap operas to be televised daily hit the air with the debut of "The Edge Of Night" and "As The World Turns" on CBS-TV.

Good Night, David-- Good Night, Chet

NBC-TV teams up Chet Huntley and David Brinkley for a nightly news show after their impressive co-anchoring of the Democratic Convention in Chicago.

Will The Real . . . Please Stand Up

Tom Poston and Kitty Carlisle head celebrity panelists on the new quiz show "To Tell The Truth." The goal is for the mystery guests to lie so convincingly that the panel believes their alleged identity.

Due To Poor Ratings, Mr. Television, Milton Berle, Loses Time Slot For First Time In Eight Years And Announces Retirement.

First "Popeye The Sailor" Cartoons Hit Television.

CBS-TV Begins Airing NFL Games On Sundays.

"Requiem For A Heavyweight" Kicks Off Outstanding Playhouse 90 Drama Series.

Nat King Cole Becomes First Black Performer To Headline Prime-Time Television Program.

TOP 10 TV SHOWS

1. *The $64,000 Question*
2. *I Love Lucy*
3. *The Ed Sullivan Show*
4. *Disneyland*
5. *The Jack Benny Show*
6. *December Bride*
7. *You Bet Your Life*
8. *Dragnet*
9. *The Millionaire*
10. *I've Got A Secret*

television

Emmy Award Winners

BEST SERIES (HALF HOUR OR LESS)
The Phil Silvers Show

BEST SERIES (ONE HOUR OR MORE)
Caesar's Hour

BEST NEW SERIES
Playhouse 90

BEST SINGLE PROGRAM
"Requiem For A Heavyweight"
Playhouse 90

BEST ACTOR
DRAMATIC SERIES
Robert Young
Father Knows Best

BEST ACTRESS
DRAMATIC SERIES
Loretta Young
The Loretta Young Show

BEST COMEDIAN
Sid Caesar
Caesar's Hour

BEST COMEDIENNE
Nanette Fabray
Caesar's Hour

BEST SUPPORTING ACTOR
Carl Reiner
Caesar's Hour

BEST SUPPORTING ACTRESS
Pat Carroll
Caesar's Hour

BEST ACTOR
SINGLE PERFORMANCE
Jack Palance
"Requiem For A Heavyweight"
Playhouse 90

BEST ACTRESS
SINGLE PERFORMANCE
Claire Trevor
"Dodsworth"
Producers' Showcase

BEST MALE PERSONALITY
Perry Como

BEST FEMALE PERSONALITY
Dinah Shore

BEST NEWS COMMENTATOR
Edward R. Murrow

BEST ORIGINAL TELEPLAY
WRITING (ONE HOUR OR MORE)
Rod Serling
"Requiem For A Heavyweight"
Playhouse 90

"**Living Color.**" 254 sq. in.* **Aldrich.** Mahogany grained finish. (21CS781) $495.   36 sq. in.* "**Personal**" **TV.** Power transformer, tilt stand, antenna. Ebony. (8PT703) $125. Other models from $99.95.

Shop Here for RCA Victor "Living

Play Santa with America's First Choice In Television! On these two pages—11 happy gift ideas for the whole family. For example…

SYMBOL OF RCA VICTOR COMPATIBLE COLOR TV

Christmas in Color! Surprise the family with a spectacular gift—RCA Victor Big Color TV. Now as low as $495—lowest price in RCA Victor history. **See natural "Living Color"**—from the delicate tint of a tea rose to the stunning tones of a Spectacular. All the colors of life!

This is BIG Color—with a big-as-life screen! Actually 254 square inches of viewable picture, on a 21-inch picture tube (overall diameter).

It's like having 2 sets in 1! For the price once paid for black-and-white alone, you see all Color shows in "Living Color" *plus* all regular programs

in crisp, clear black-and-white. It's RCA Victor *Compatible* Color TV.

So easy to tune, a child can do it. Turn two knobs and the screen blossoms out in Color.

Choose from 10 models—masterpieces of modern or traditional styling. From a table model to luxurious consoles—it's Color TV's first complete line!

Or give a TV Original—new shapes, new sizes, new styles, new convenience in black-and-white TV. New "*Personal*" TV starts at $99.95—smartest, smallest TV ever! And it's a *full-fledged* TV set with sturdy case and regular power transformer.

"PERSONAL"

Lowest priced RCA Victor TV. 36 sq. in.* screen, handle, power transformer, antenna connection. Ebony. (8PT7011) $99.95.

TABLE TV

Big-screen TV—budget price. "High-Sharp-and-Easy" tuning. 261 sq. in.* *Dixon*. Ebony finish. (21T715) $219.95.

SWIVEL

Built-in phono-jack for record player! 261 sq. in.* *Enfield*. Mahogany grained finish. (21T738) $299.95.

ROLLAROUND

Glide it from room to room! 261 sq. in.* *Ardmore Deluxe*. Limed oak grained finish. (21D721) $269.95.

LOWBOY

Fine furniture—2 speakers. 261 sq. in.* *Raeburn*. Smart limed oak grained finish. (21T741) $339.95.

LUXURY CONSOLE

3 speakers! Big, big screen. 329 sq. in.* *Brantley Deluxe*. Mahogany figured finish. (24D770) $475.

"LIVING COLOR"

"Living Color" picture. "Window Knob" indicator. 254 sq. in.* *Westcott*. Limed oak grained finish. (21CT785) $595.

"LIVING COLOR"

Handsome new lowboy. Easy "Color-Quick" tuning. 254 sq. in.* *Dartmouth*. Mahogany grained finish. (21CT786) $650.

"LIVING COLOR"

3-speaker Panoramic Sound. Provincial styling. *Wingate Deluxe*. Genuine maple veneers and solids. (21CD799) $850.

Color"—and TV Originals From $99⁹⁵

3-Speaker Panoramic Sound in most Deluxe models. Amazing "you are there" realism—finest sound to go with TV's finest picture!
"High-Sharp-and-Easy" tuning. Tune standing up. RCA "Magic Brain" remote TV control available for most models (optional, extra).
Whatever you want in TV—for yourself or for a gift—RCA Victor has it. And remember: ask your dealer about easy budget terms on RCA Victor black-and-white or Big Color TV.

Manufacturer's nationally advertised VHF list prices shown. Prices and specifications subject to change. UHF optional, extra (not available on *Personal*). Some sets slightly higher far West and South. Most models available in Canada.

At your service: RCA Victor Factory Service Contracts available in most areas but only to RCA Victor TV owners. Special low-cost

1-year contract on *"Personal"* or portable—only $14.95. Special 90-day Big Color TV contract only $39.95.

SEE TOP SHOWS IN COLOR and black-and-white over NBC-TV: "The Perry Como Show," Sat., Dec. 15; "Saturday Color Carnival," Dec. 22. Co-sponsored by RCA Victor.

RADIO CORPORATION OF AMERICA

"THE GIFT THAT KEEPS ON GIVING"

*Square inches of viewable picture area	36	108	254	261	329
Picture tube, overall diagonal or diameter	8"	14"	21"	21"	24"

art

Emilio Greco's Statue Of Pinocchio, Honoring The Author Of The Classic Tale, Carlo Lorenzini, Wins Over 82 Others In A Sculpture Competition In Ancona, Italy.

Young British Painters Swing Back To Realism And Are Dubbed "The Kitchen Sink School."

Claude Monet's Water Lily Paintings Are Acquired By The Museum Of Modern Art And The Art Institute Of Chicago, Thrusting The Great French Impressionist Painter Into Prominence.

The Frank Lloyd Wright Designed Los Angeles Municipal Art Gallery Is Dedicated And Construction On His Guggenheim Museum Begins In New York.

Richard Lippold's Commissioned Piece, "Variation Within A Sphere, No. 10: The Sun" Goes On Exhibition In New York's Metropolitan Museum of Art. The Piece Is Constructed With More Than Two Miles Of Wire And 14,000 Hand-Welded Joints.

Sam Francis, 32-Year Old Ex-GI, Becomes The Most Well Known American Painter In Europe, Specializing In Exploration In The Quality Of Light.

VENICE BIENNALE PRIZES
PAINTING: Jacques Villon (80 Year Old French Cubist)
SCULPTURE: Lynn Chadwick (Great Britain)
DRAWING: Aldemir Martins (Brazil)

NEW PAINTINGS
John Bratby ......*"A Painter's Credo"*
Lynn Chadwick ...*"Teddy Boy And Girl"*
Bernard Buffet ...*"Self-portrait"*

NEW SCULPTURE
Barbara Hepworth *"Orpheus"*

Prehistoric Art Discovered In Caves In Dordogne, France

An Original "Madonna And Child" By Leonardo da Vinci Valued At $1 Million Is Found In A New York Antique Shop.

"Composition #3" By Russian Pioneer Abstractionist Wassily Kandinsky, Painted In 1914, Is Finally Shown.

With The Growing Interest In American Paintings, Museum Directors Have Turned To The American Impressionists, Buying Such Works As Childe Hassam's "Church At Old Lyme, Conn.," Maurice Prendergast's "Sunset And Sea Fog" And John Twachtman's "Fishing Boats At Gloucester."

London Critics Give Less Than Hospitable Reception To Modern U.S. Art Exhibition On Display At The Tate Gallery, Finding Works By Jackson Pollock, Clyfford Still, Willem de Kooning, Mark Rothko And Robert Motherwell Disquieting And Nightmarish.

Painter Charles Burchfield Lauded By Critics And Dubbed The Greatest Living U.S. Watercolorist Despite His Opinion That Most People Are Bored Or Indifferent About Nature, The Subject Of His Works.

New York's National Academy Of Design Awards The Benjamin Altman Figure Painting Prize To Morton Roberts For His Work Entitled "Bar And Grill."

The United States Participates In The 28th Venice Biennale With An Exhibition Assembled By The Art Institute Of Chicago Entitled "American Artists Paint The City" Consisting Of Works By Edward Hopper, John Marin, Stuart Davis And Jackson Pollock.

PASSINGS

JACKSON POLLOCK, Pioneer Abstract Expressionist, Dies At 44 In An Automobile Accident.

MAURICE UTRILLO, French Painter, Dies At 71.

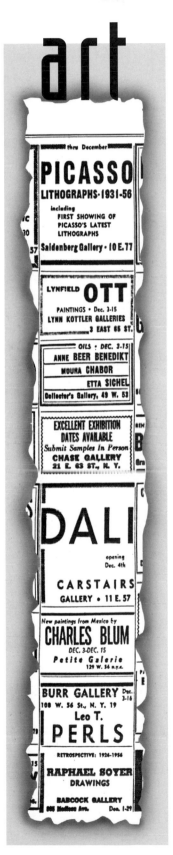

1956

books

A Charmed Life
MARY MCCARTHY

A Family Party
Ten North Frederick
JOHN O'HARA

A Historian's Approach To
Religion
ARNOLD TOYNBEE

A Season To Beware
WILLIAM DUBOIS

A Single Pebble
JOHN HERSEY

A Walk On The Wild Side
NELSON ALGREN

Adonis And The Alphabet
ALDOUS HUXLEY

All Honorable Men
DAVID KARP

All The Kingdoms
Of The Earth
HOKE NORRIS

Amrita
R. PRAWER JHABVALA

Anglo-Saxon Attitudes
ANGUS WILSON

Bang The Drum Slowly
MARK HARRIS

Boon Island
KENNETH ROBERTS

Comfort Me With Apples
PETER DE VRIES

Diamonds Are Forever
IAN FLEMING

Don't Go Near The Water
WILLIAM BRINKLEY

Essays On The Sociology
Of Culture
KARL MANHEIM

Field Of Vision
WRIGHT MORRIS

Freedom Or Death
NIKOS KAZANTZAKIS

Helen Keller: Sketch
For A Portrait
VAN WYCK BROOKS

H.M.S. Ulysses
ALISTAIR MACLEAN

Howl And Other Poems
ALLEN GINSBERG

Imperial Woman
PEARL BUCK

Lady Sings The Blues
BILLIE HOLIDAY

Lucy Crown
IRWIN SHAW

Men And Power, 1917
LORD BEAVERBROOK

Notes Of A Native Son
JAMES BALDWIN

Nuni
**JOHN HOWARD
GRIFFIN**

O Beulah Land
**MARY LEE
SETTLE**

PULITZER PRIZES

BIOGRAPHY

TALBOT F. HAMLIN
Benjamin Henry Latrobe

FICTION

MACKINLAY KANTOR
Andersonville

POETRY

ELIZABETH BISHOP
"Poems, North And South"

WHAT A YEAR IT WAS!

books

Obscenity And The Law
NORMAN ST. JOHN-STEVAS

Paper Dolls
LAURA BEHELER

Peyton Place
GRACE METALIOUS

Profiles In Courage
JOHN F. KENNEDY

Seize The Day
SAUL BELLOW

Speak To The Winds
RUTH MOORE

The Atlantic Battle Won
SAMUEL ELIOT MORISON

The Color Curtain
RICHARD WRIGHT

The End Of The Track
ANDREW GARVE

The Horse Soldiers
HAROLD SINCLAIR

The King Of Paris
GUY ENDORE

The Last Hurrah
EDWIN O'CONNOR

The Malefactors
CAROLINE GORDON

The Man Who Studied Yoga
NORMAN MAILER

The Man Who Was Not With It
HERBERT GOLD

The Marble Orchard
MARGARET BOYLEN

The Ninth Wave
EUGENE BURDICK

The Nun's Story
KATHRYN HULME

The Organization Man
W.H. WHYTE

The Outsider
COLIN WILSON

The Quiet American
GRAHAM GREENE

The Search For Bridey Murphy
MOREY BERNSTEIN

The Theme Is Freedom
JOHN DOS PASSOS

The Tribe That Lost Its Head
NICHOLAS MONSARRAT

The Young Lincoln
STERLING NORTH

This Is Our World
LOUIS FISCHER

Walk Through The Valley
BORDEN DEAL

What I Think
ADLAI STEVENSON

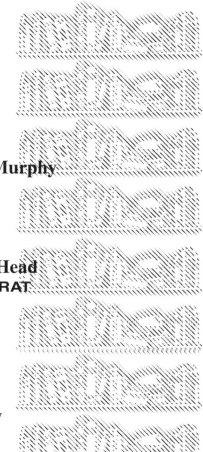

PASSINGS

A.A. MILNE, Creator Of "Winnie the Pooh", Dies At 74.

H.L. MENCKEN, Author And Editor, Dies At 75.

GEORGE TERRY DUNLAP, Co-Founder Of Grosset & Dunlap, Dies At 92.

WHAT A YEAR IT WAS!

1956

classical music

*V*ienna State Opera Gets New Musical Director – Herbert von Karajan.

*A*ustria Celebrates Mozart On Bicentennial.

*O*pera Premiere: Douglas Moore, "The Ballad Of Baby Doe."

*G*ian Carlo Menotti Debuts His Opera, "The Unicorn, The Gorgon And The Manticore" In Washington, D.C.

*W*illiam Bergama's Opera "The Wife Of Martin Guerre" Opens In New York.

*M*aria Callas Debuts At The Metropolitan Opera In Bellini's "Norma".

• Lily Pons Celebrates 25th Anniversary Of Metropolitan Opera Debut.

• Self-Exiled Spanish Cellist, Pablo Casals, Announces He Will Make His Home In Puerto Rico.

• Mattiwilda Dobbs Debuts As Gilda In "Rigoletto" With The New York Metropolitan Opera, Becoming The Third Negro* Singer To Be Featured At The Metropolitan And The First Negro To Sing A Non-Negro Romantic Lead.

*Negro was the commonly used term in 1956.

dance • dance • dance • dance • dance • dance

ON • OUR • TOES

New Ballet: Humphrey Searle, "Noctambules"

Ballerina Margot Fonteyn Is Appointed Dame Commander Of The Order Of The British Empire.

Sadler's Wells Ballet Renamed The Royal Ballet.

WHAT A YEAR IT WAS!

BROADWAY OPENINGS

theatre

Terence Rattigan's "Separate Tables" Opens In New York.

Bernstein's Musical Comedy "Candide" Opens In New York.

Alan Jay Lerner & Frederick Loewe Open "My Fair Lady" In New York.

PLAYS

A Hatful Of Rain ◆ Auntie Mame
A View From The Bridge
Bells Are Ringing ◆ Desk Set
Fallen Angels ◆ Li'l Abner
Long Day's Journey Into Night
Look Back In Anger ◆ Middle Of The Night
No Time For Sergeants ◆ Richard III
The Chalk Garden ◆ The Great Sebastians
The Lark
The Matchmaker
The Most Happy Fella
Tiger At The Gates
Waiting For Godot
Will Success Spoil Rock Hunter?

"THE ICEMAN COMETH" BY EUGENE O'NEILL OPENS AT CIRCLE-IN-THE-SQUARE IN NEW YORK.

ON BROADWAY

Candide
Irra Pettina

Fallen Angels
Nancy Walker

My Fair Lady
From left: Robert Coote, Rex Harrison, Julie Andrews, Michael King and Cathleen Nesbitt

WHAT A YEAR IT WAS!

A View From The Bridge
*From left: Gloria Marlowe,
Van Heflin and
Eileen Heckart*

No Time For Sergeants
From left: Roddy McDowall and Andy Griffith

Bells Are Ringing
*From left:
Judy Holliday and
Peter Gennaro*

1956

"PORGY & BESS" PLAYS LENINGRAD

The first American musical troupe to ever visit Leningrad performs "Porgy & Bess," receiving a 10-minute standing ovation from a wildly enthusiastic audience.

Brecht's Berliner Ensemble Visits England.

BERTOLT BRECHT, prolific playwright including "The Threepenny Opera" and "Mother Courage And Her Children", dies at 58.

TONY AWARDS

Dramatic Actor:
Paul Muni, Inherit The Wind

Dramatic Actress:
Julie Harris, The Lark

Play:
The Diary Of Anne Frank

Musical Actor:
Ray Walston, Damn Yankees

Musical Actress:
Gwen Verdon,
Damn Yankees

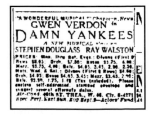

Musical:
Damn Yankees

A Streetcar Named... I'm Out Of Here

After attending several painful performances of "A Streetcar Named Desire" starring Tallulah Bankhead and her gross misinterpretation of Blanche Dubois, Tennessee Williams could not stand his play being ruined and left town to avoid hearing anything else about the nightly spectacle.

PULITZER PRIZE

Frances Goodrich & Albert Hackett

The Diary Of Anne Frank

New York DRAMA CRITICS CIRCLE AWARDS

BEST PLAY
The Diary Of Anne Frank,
Frances Goodrich & Albert Hackett
BEST FOREIGN PLAY
Tiger At The Gates, **Christopher Fry**
BEST MUSICAL
My Fair Lady, **Alan Jay Lerner & Frederick Loewe**

WHAT A YEAR IT WAS!

DISASTERS

29 DIE, 142 HURT IN CALIFORNIA TRAIN WRECK

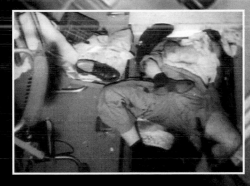

Most of the victims, predominantly servicemen on furlough, are pinned in the wreckage.

Hundreds of feet of track are ripped up as a Flyer overturns on a curve.

Investigators are on the scene immediately to try to determine the cause of this terrible disaster.

1956

Devastating Twisters Rip Through The Midwest

Hudsonville, Michigan is worst hit by a two-day series of storms that strike 14 states in the nation's midsection.

With 13 dead in Hudsonville, the rest of the residents escape with their lives and not much else.

WHAT A YEAR IT WAS!

Winter storm batters Canary Islands

Torrential rains cause landslides destroying 57 homes and washing out bridges.

Worst Air Disaster In Commercial Aviation History Occurs Over The Grand Canyon As Two U.S. Planes Carrying 128 People Collide.

- Collapse of shrine wall kills 125 during New Year's celebrations at Niigata, Japan.

- Cold weather and storms result in $10 million damage to Florida crops.

- Blizzard and intense cold wave in Western Europe kill 1,000 and cause crop damage estimated at $2 billion.

- 162 deaths and $150 million property damage result from 4-day snowstorm in Northeastern U.S.

- 30 are killed by bomb accidentally dropped from Thai Air Force plane.

- Earthquake (7.7 on Richter scale) in northern Afghanistan kills 2,000.

- Venezuelan Super-Constellation crashes in Atlantic off Asbury Park, NJ – all 74 aboard killed.

- 208 firemen hurt during fire in abandoned Wanamaker's store in New York City.

- 2,161 Chinese reported killed by floods caused by typhoon Wanda.

- 262 killed in coal mine fire in Marcinelle, Belgium.

President Eisenhower Announces Steps To Help Ease Acute Distress In U.S. Drought Areas.

Disaster At Sea

The Italian luxury liner "Andrea Doria" sinks after a collision with Sweden's "Stockholm" in a crowded shipping lane near New York.

Andrea Doria

The "Ile de France", which headed the rescue work of 10 vessels, steams into New York with 700 survivors.

New York's piers are the scene of joyful reunions. Tragically, 50 had died but a major disaster was averted.

1956

Floods Threaten Yuba City

The Feather River menaces the levees guarding Yuba City, California.

Engineers closely watch the rising water and phone the alarm as the crest rises.

Weary residents prepare to evacuate for the third time in six weeks.

Eisenhower Declares California Major Disaster Area As A Result Of Devastating Flooding.

Residents trying to dry out from the previous flood, which cost 34 lives and $179 million, form a motorcade to take refuge on higher ground.

Winter Storm Strikes Holland

Winter moves in on Holland with a raging snowstorm.

Spectators look at a car that skidded into one of the canals.

Amsterdam is particularly hard hit by the fall of 20 inches, which brings the railroad to a virtual standstill.

Nova Scotia Crippled By Flood

A sudden thaw coupled with rain brings heavy flooding to Nova Scotia.

Near Halifax, hundreds of cars are lost as the water rises higher and higher.

Minor streams become raging torrents, sweeping away everything in their path.

Bridges are undermined and damage runs into the tens of millions.

The Teen Look

girls

- Oversized men's shirt with rolled up jeans
- Penny loafers or black-and-white saddle shoes
- Hair: ponytail

boys

- Blue jeans with penny loafers or black-and-white saddle shoes
- Hair: the Elvis Presley look – greasy ducktail and sideburns
- Ivy League Look

FASHION

1956

The World's Beautiful Women

Tenley Albright

Anita Ekberg

Greta Garbo

Ava Gardner

Grace Kelly

Gina Lollobrigida

Anna Magnani

Maharanee of Jaipur

Kim Novak

Grace Paley

Sharon Kay Ritchie

Eva Marie Saint

Elizabeth Taylor

Jeanne Vanderbilt

PASSINGS

Hattie Carnegie, Designer To The Rich And Famous, Dies At 69 Of Cancer.

I'll take romance...

The return to the "Romantic Look" brings grace, charm and beauty to women's fashion this year with designer collections incorporating yards and yards of extravagant clinging or floating fabrics like white sheer silk dresses embroidered in pink and gold or pastel dotted organdy gowns with winged sleeves, trimmed with pink ribbons and roses on the bodice. The silhouette is softened through the use of draping and a profusion of color is generously used, moving away from stark simplicity to the visual opulence brought to life by the stunning costumes seen in "My Fair Lady" reflecting the late Edwardian period (1906-1912).

Capes are seen everywhere – with collars, hoods, or shawls, and some trimmed with that new status symbol fur – mink.

THE BASICS OF AN ELEGANT WARDROBE

(Simplicity Is The Key)

1. **Three Basic Elements**
   a. **A Suit**
   b. **A Sheath**
   c. **A Narrow, Décolleté Cocktail Dress**
2. **Real Jewels Or Copies Of Old Ones**
3. **Contrasting Colors For Bags & Hats**
4. **Slender Heels, Not Too High**
5. **Gloves** *(8-buttons vs. Shorter Length)*

WHAT A YEAR IT WAS!

The new, new, new...

"Lady Ronson"
ELECTRIC SHAVER

Keeps your legs and underarms smooth as slipper satin...and it's fun to use!

How *ridiculous* to risk old-fashioned razors that leave nasty little nicks, or razor-burned skin! It's so safe and *simple* to "defuzz" with "LADY RONSON", the chic little shaver with *two sides*: one to give legs a slipper-satin finish...one to keep underarms smooth as a baby's! And with "LADY RONSON", you shave *far less frequently*, stay hair-free days *longer!* You'll adore it!

It's the glamour gift of the year!

Blush Pink

Blue Heaven

Turquoise

Black Magic

Set with a make-believe diamond!

14⁹⁵
(complete with case)

RONSON® *maker of the world's greatest lighters and electric shavers*

COSTUME: TINA LESER   RONSON CORPORATION, NEWARK Z. N. J.; TORONTO, ONT.; LONDON, ENG.

The Don Loper Collection

Designer Don Loper escorts his favorite model Marilyn for a day at the Beverly Hills Hotel. She wears one of his creations – a two-piece suit designed to travel.

Another piece in his collection is this gold linen ensemble with polka dot silk and mandarin side slit coat accessorized with a fishnet basket purse and a large piped straw cartwheel hat.

A mandarin ensemble over blue taffeta set off with a glamorous harlequin bow.

This evening gown in the new flamenco length is called "Symphony" and is made of re-embroidered mauve lace with a graceful, flowing draped sash panel.

And for the hourglass look, here's Loper's "Can-Can" evening gown, hand-painted lace over layers of tulle.

WHAT A YEAR IT WAS!

1956 ADVERTISEMENT

YESTERDAY a dream...**TODAY** a dream room!

It's this easy with speedy *Super Kem-Tone*

THE DE LUXE LATEX WALL PAINT

It's a wonderful feeling! Your dream becomes a brand-new room in just one day with quick, ready-to-use Super Kem-Tone! Velvet-rich, rubber-tough, it goes on easily over plaster, wallpaper, paint, wood, brick or wallboard without brush marks. Dries within an hour, too. Yet Super Kem-Tone costs so little to use . . . one gallon will do the walls of an average room. Give your own dream a try with Super Kem-Tone . . . then you'll know why it's the world's most widely used wall paint.

Kem-Glo® alkyd enamel matches Super Kem-Tone color for color. It's the favorite enamel for kitchens, bathrooms and all wood-work in the home. Kem-Glo flows on smooth-ly . . . no undercoater needed . . . looks and washes like baked enamel.

SUPER KEM-TONE $5.89 gallon (Deep tones $6.19 a gallon). KEM-GLO $2.69 a quart.

Wide range of lovely new colors to choose from!

Easy to apply with Roller-Koater® or brush!

Guaranteed washable, or your money back!

THE SHERWIN-WILLIAMS CO.

In Principal Cities from Coast to Coast
Super Kem-Tone and Kem-Glo are also made and distributed by:
Acme Quality Paints, Inc., Detroit • W. W. Lawrence & Co., Pittsburgh • The Lowe Brothers Co., Dayton • John Lucas & Co., Inc., Philadelphia • The Martin-Senour Co., Chicago • Rogers Paint Products, Inc., Detroit.

FREE! "The Home Decorator" . . . 44 colorful pages full of wonderful decorating ideas. Write Sherwin-Williams, 1255 Midland Bldg., Cleveland 1, Ohio.

141

1956

Christian Dior Fashion

The Dior collection features a return to the picture hat.

A hint of Casablanca in this multi-colored striped silk with its hood and flowing lines.

This sports outfit is a brilliant red linen which buttons from neckline to hemline.

Pink brocade evening coats are accented by deep pockets, bows, and mauve lining.

This wraparound jacket lined with millium will insure staying cool.

Sparkling earrings and bracelet make this the height of fashion.

Helena Barbieri Unveils Feminine Evening Wear

A lace and embroidered sheer cocktail creation is set off with a mutation mink.

The Dresden figurine look is captured in this beautiful pin-tucked sheer that folds into a cascade of pleats topped off with an autumn haze capelet.

1956 ADVERTISEMENT

Gowns by Bergdorf Goodman

Ordinarily, when a motorist purchases a new Cadillac, he does so for pride and for satisfaction . . . and for the personal happiness the car will bring him. But it is reassuring to know that—if he preferred—he could choose the "car of cars" solely on the basis of economy. For it is a documented fact that Cadillac, with all its great beauty and luxury and performance, is among the most practical of all motor cars to own and to operate. If you are currently considering the purchase of any new motor car, we earnestly suggest that you visit us soon for a personal inspection and demonstration of this latest Cadillac creation. We will be happy to show you why this is such a wonderful time to make the move . . . both for pride *and* for practicality!

YOUR CADILLAC DEALER

Cadillac

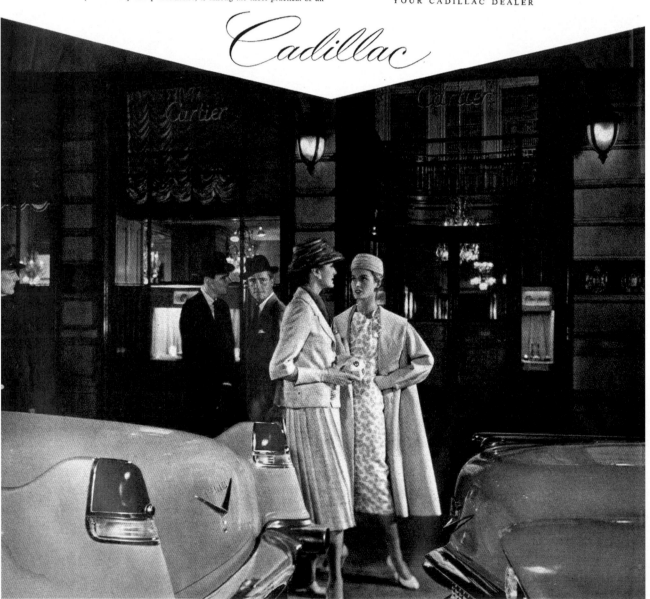

Having Your Easter Hat And Eating It Too!

Not only do these Easter bonnets look delicious, they *are* delicious as the pastry chef whipped them up out of powdered sugar and egg whites.

How many calories do you suppose are in this little bonnet?

Jantzen Kharafleece Sweaters

The luxury in the fabric is Vicara

BRAND ZEIN FIBERS

Getting a rush on every campus—fall's new Kharafleece sweaters lavishly enriched with lush *Vicara* fiber. Glad news you may not find in a textbook—not only does this luxury fiber bring a soft beauty to the blend, it also keeps you blissfully comfortable! Because *Vicara* fiber is absorbent, you never have that unpleasant cold and clammy feeling. Your new Kharafleece sweater washes easier…no blocking, no shrinking, no stretching. And it resists soiling longer… *Vicara* fiber is anti-static, simply doesn't attract lint or dirt. Its gentle, well-bred good looks will last…there'll be no unsightly matting, no "fuzzing up". Most of all, you'll revel in its rich texture, a heavenly touch that sweaters never had before…a precious gift of luxury that only *Vicara* fiber bestows on the nicest sweaters you'll ever own. Remember the name: Kharafleece sweaters by Jantzen!

Jantzen Kharafleece *knitwear is yours in an opulent range of colors at fine stores everywhere. Hand-washable, mothproof, wrinkle-resistant. Girl's sweater, about 11.00. Skirt, about 14.00. Men's sweaters, about 12.00. The golfer shirt (about 13.00) and sheath dress (about 30.00) are also in wonderful Kharafleece. Vicara brand zein fibers are made by Virginia-Carolina Chemical Corporation 99 Park Avenue, New York 16, New York*

SPORTS

Thousands of fans gather to cheer their favorite team.

Baseball

Yankees And Dodgers Battle For World Series Crown

Mickey Mantle climaxes the winning season capturing the triple crown.

A thrilling moment for the victorious Yankees.

Yankee pitcher Don Larsen makes baseball history.

WHAT A YEAR IT WAS!

Baseball Hall Of Famer Connie Mack Dies

Comedy Team **Abbott & Costello's** "Who's On First" Baseball Routine Is Enshrined In Baseball Hall Of Fame.

Cornelius McGillicuddy, known throughout his 70-year baseball career as Connie Mack, is pictured with Babe Ruth and other Hall of Famers.

Connie will be remembered not only for his baseball skills but for the character and integrity he typified.

WHAT DO YA MEAN YOU DIDN'T LIKE THAT CATCH!

Boston Red Sox's Ted Williams Fined $5,000 After He Spit At Fans And Reporters During A Game Played Against The Yankees.

1956

Rookie Of The Year:

LOU APARICIO
(Chicago White Sox)

FRANK ROBINSON
(Cincinnati Redlegs)

Baseball's Yearly Schedule Is Set In Braille For The First Time, Appearing In The May 7 Issue Of The "Weekly News", The Only Newspaper For The Blind In The English-Speaking World.

Player Of The Year:
MICKEY MANTLE

New York Yankees Take Their 17th World Series Victory By Beating Brooklyn 4-3.

DALE LONG, Pittsburgh First Baseman, Sets Major League Record By Hitting A Home Run In Eight Consecutive Games.

DON LARSEN Of The New York Yankees, Pitches The First Perfect Major League Baseball Game In 34 Years And The First No-Hit Game In World Series History.

WHAT A YEAR IT WAS!

THE BEL AIR BEAUVILLE—*4 doors, 9 passengers, interior finish in washable vinyl and nylon-faced pattern cloth.*

Seats a whole baseball team

It's one of <u>6</u> sprightly

THE "TWO-TEN" HANDYMAN
2 doors, 6 passengers, all-vinyl interior.

THE DISTINCTIVE. LUXURIOUS NOMAD
2 doors, 6 passengers.

THE "TWO-TEN" TOWNSMAN
4 doors, 6 passengers, loads of cargo space.

In place of baseball players, of course, it could be other people. Friends of yours, for instance, assorted small fry, or visiting dignitaries.

Anyway, there's room for 3 on each seat, 9 in all. (A separate section of the center seat folds down to allow rear seat passengers to get in and out easily and gracefully.) And there's even space left over for baseball bats or baggage.

If you're joining the fast-growing station wagon family, be sure to look these new Chevrolets over. They're very good looking, as you see. All of them have fine, sturdy and quiet Fisher Bodies. All offer you an engine choice of V8 or 6, and all the power features anybody would want. And all of them pack Chevrolet's special brand of performance that breaks records on Pikes Peak and makes your own driving easier, safer and more pleasant.

Color and interior choices are wide, practical and unusually handsome. We'll be happy to help you make your selection.

SEE YOUR CHEVROLET DEALER

beautifully !

new Chevrolet station wagons

THE "ONE-FIFTY" HANDYMAN
2 doors, 6 passengers, versatile and thrifty.

THE "TWO-TEN" BEAUVILLE
4 doors, 9 passengers.

CHEVROLET

Traffic-test it— it's a beautiful thing to handle!

1956

FOOTBALL

EAST MEETS WEST IN PRO BOWL GAME

Christiansen scores a touch-down for the West.

Top players in the National League meet in the Pro Bowl Game. Christiansen of the Lions sets the stage with a run back of 103 yards.

LeBaron of the Redskins throws a pass that is intercepted by Jim David of the West All-Stars.

Hearst scores – making the final score East 31, West 30.

Heisman Trophy Winner: Paul Hornung (Notre Dame Quarterback)

Michigan State Beats UCLA 17-14 In Rose Bowl Competition.

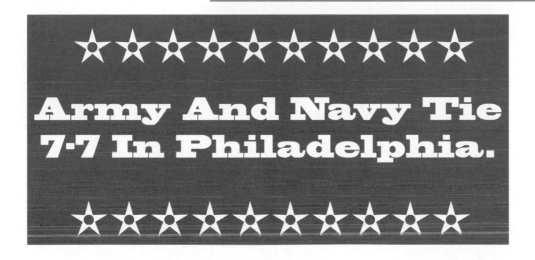

★★★★★★★★★★★★

Army And Navy Tie 7-7 In Philadelphia.

★★★★★★★★★★★★

Best U.S. College Football Team: Oklahoma

New York Giants Beat Chicago Bears 47-7, Winning NFL Championship.

FOOTBALL COACH OF THE YEAR: BOWDEN WYATT, UNIVERSITY OF TENNESSEE

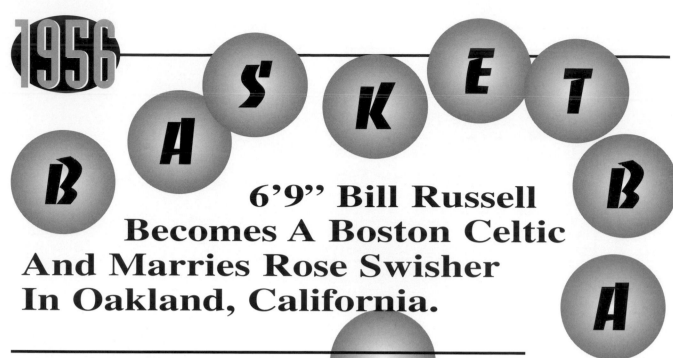

BASKETBALL

6'9" Bill Russell
Becomes A Boston Celtic
And Marries Rose Swisher
In Oakland, California.

Philadelphia Warriors Beat Fort Wayne Pistons 4-1 For NBA Championship.

San Francisco Whips Iowa 83-71, Winning NCAA Championship

Most Valuable Player: Bob Pettit (St. Louis Hawks)

Rookie Of The Year: Maurice Stokes (Rochester Royals)

1956

Son And Grandson Of Derby Winners

Upholds The Family Honor

HORSE RACING

RACING FORM

In one of the richest derbies ever, and one of the most thrilling in the history of the Kentucky classic, D. Erb rides "Needles" to victory, moving from 16th place. "Needles" also wins the Belmont Stakes.

GOLF MASTERS GOLF TOURNAMENT IN AUGUSTA, GA

Ken Venturi's lead by 8 strokes collapses in the final round as rival Jack Burke climaxes a great rally to hole out one stroke, winning the title and $6,000 purse.

Venturi congratulates Burke after a stunning match.

Burke puts on the green coat of victory.

Spectators gather to watch the competition between Ken Venturi and Jack Burke.

The world mourns the passing of Babe Didrikson Zaharias, considered to be the greatest woman athlete of all time.

Babe's warm-hearted sportsmanship never failed during her gallant 3-year fight against cancer.

champions

U.S. Open	Cary Middlecoff
Masters	Jack Burke
British Open . .	Peter Thomson

NATIONAL AMATEUR GOLF

In the National Amateur Tournament held at Lake Forest, defending title holder Harvey Ward holed out five and four to become the first two-time amateur champ in 21 years.

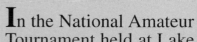
WHAT A YEAR IT WAS!

1956

Indy 500-Mile Memorial Day Classic

A series of chilling accidents knock out 12 cars from the race, but fortunately there is no loss of life.

33 cars line up for start of the annual classic.

Red-headed Pat Flaherty emerges the victor.

So Refreshing!
Never bitter – never harsh!

No other beer refreshes like Schlitz, nor gives such satisfaction and pleasure. Here is a beer so fine it made a city famous!

Brewed for quality, never for price, Schlitz is preferred (and bought) by more people than any other beer, at *any* price.

THE BEER THAT MADE MILWAUKEE FAMOUS

© 1956—Jos. Schlitz Brewing Company, Milwaukee, Wis.,
Brooklyn, N. Y., Los Angeles, Calif.

Diving Trials

Pat McCormick takes top high diving spot and goes on to win at the Summer Olympics in Melbourne.

Barbara Sue Gilders takes second place.

Jeanne Stunyo finishes in third place.

Ten horses of the United States Olympic Jumping Team are loaded aboard a trans-Atlantic plane for their trip to Stockholm for the June competition.

The valuable steeds are secured in their stalls for a long 15-hour flight.

The equestrian team gets ready to board with high hopes of bringing home an Olympic victory.

Horses and riders representing 19 nations gather to compete in the Olympic steeplechase on a rain-drenched, perilous 22-mile course.

OLYMPIC STEEPLECHASE TRIALS HELD OUTSIDE OF STOCKHOLM

45 official hazards send six riders to the hospital with 11 teams failing to finish.

One badly injured horse had to be destroyed in this memorable but not inspiring sport event.

WINTER
OLYMPICS

AMERICA SWEEPS ARTISTIC EVENTS IN WINTER OLYMPICS HELD IN CORTINA D'AMPEZZO, ITALY

Tenley Albright, still in pain from a recent leg injury, shows courage to match her gracefulness.

Hayes Alan Jenkins gives a stylistic performance on the ice.

The Champions: Hayes Alan Jenkins and Tenley Albright.

With Soviet athletes dominating the Winter Olympics, the 500 meter speed skating is an easy win for the Iron Curtain Team.

Austria's domination was visible on the giant slalom with Tony Sailer easily taking the trail that plummets downward for almost two miles through 69 gates with a vertical drop of one mile to the finish line, winning the gold medal.

Tony Sailer wins the slalom, giant slalom and the downhill on one of Europe's toughest, trickiest slopes.

WINNERS

FIGURE SKATING:
      Men's: *Hayes Alan Jenkins (USA)*
      Women's: *Tenley Albright (USA)*
      Pairs: *Elisabeth Schwartz & Kurt Oppelt (Austria)*

SPEED SKATING:
      Men's 500 Meters: *Evgeniy Grishin (USSR)*
      Men's 10,000 Meters: *Sigvard Ericsson (Sweden)*

ALPINE SKIING:
      Men's Downhill: *Anton Sailer (Austria)*
      Women's Downhill: *Madeleine Berthod (Switzerland)*

DECEMBER: 1956 Summer Olympic Games Opened By Duke Of Edinburgh In Melbourne, Australia.

W I N N E R S

MEN'S TRACK & FIELD

100 Meter Run: Robert Morrow (USA)

400 Meter Run: Charles Jenkins (USA)

1500 Meter Run: Ron Delany (Ireland)

5000 Meter Run: Vladimir Kuts (USSR)

High Jump: Charles Dumas (USA)

Pole Vault: Robert Richards (USA)

WOMEN'S SWIMMING

100 Meter Freestyle: Dawn Fraser (Australia)

400 Meter Freestyle: Lorraine Crapp (Australia)

100 Meter Butterfly: Shelley Mann (USA)

Platform Diving: Patricia McCormick (USA)

Springboard Diving: Patricia McCormick (USA)

SHELLEY MANN

FAMOUS BIRTHS

- LARRY BIRD
  - BJORN BORG
- SUGAR RAY LEONARD
  - JOE MONTANA
- MARTINA NAVRATILOVA

Track & Field

John Landy (left) congratulates Jim Bailey after his historic run.

Track and field history is made in Los Angeles Coliseum as Australia's John Landy, making his American debut, is upset by fellow Aussie Jim Bailey in a sensational race.

First 4-Minute Mile Run In The United States

Charlie Dumas, 19, clears the 7-foot mark in the high jump, an accomplishment comparable to the first 4-minute mile.

WHAT A YEAR IT WAS!

ICE SKATING

WORLD CHAMPIONSHIP

Men: *Hayes Alan Jenkins (U.S.)*
Women: *Carol Heiss (U.S.)*

U.S. NATIONAL

MEN: *Hayes Alan Jenkins*
WOMEN: *Tenley Albright*

CANADIAN NATIONAL

MEN: *Charles Snelling*
WOMEN: *Carole Jane Pachl*

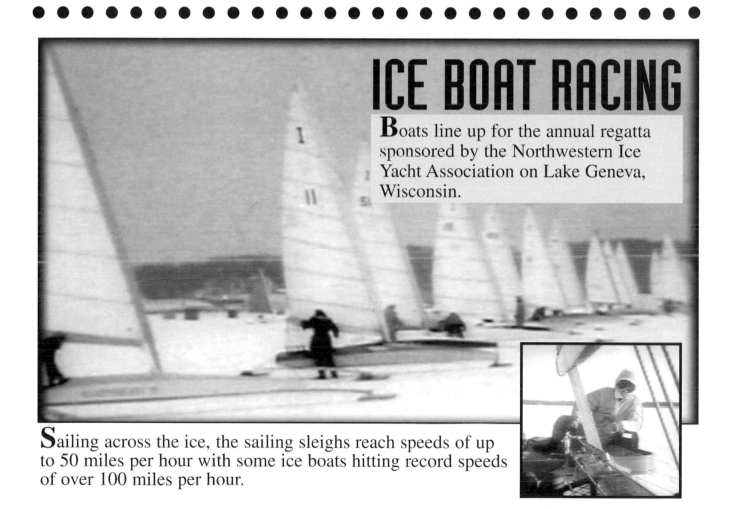

ICE BOAT RACING

Boats line up for the annual regatta sponsored by the Northwestern Ice Yacht Association on Lake Geneva, Wisconsin.

Sailing across the ice, the sailing sleighs reach speeds of up to 50 miles per hour with some ice boats hitting record speeds of over 100 miles per hour.

HOCKEY
Montreal Canadiens Beat Detroit Red Wings 4-1 For Stanley Cup Championship

1956

k a y a k

sea going slalom in Germany

The quaint old mountain village of Monschau near the Belgian border is the site of the first seagoing slalom of the season.

The surging current slams this athlete into a wall.

Kayak skippers from five nations compete in the cold, rough waters.

The chilled but thrilled winners.

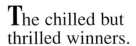

Austrian and Polish bikers compete in Vienna.

20,000 horrified fans watch as luck runs out for one of the daredevils who meets a fiery death after crashing into another biker wedging himself in a stairwell.

The second biker crawls to safety and the race continues.

Motorcycle Racing

The Annual Hill Climb Sponsored By The Lewis & Clark Motorcycle Club Gets Under Way In Lewiston, Idaho.

CHAMPIONS

ATHLETE OF THE YEAR

Male . . . . Mickey Mantle (Baseball)
Female . . . . Pat McCormick (Diving)

TOUR DE FRANCE . . .Roger Walkowiak

TENNIS

Althea Gibson, First Negro* Player To Tour The Major World Amateur Tennis Circuit, Places Second In Women's Singles Tennis Championship At Forest Hills, NY After Capturing Titles In France, Italy And Great Britain.

**Negro was the commonly used term in 1956.*

TENNIS CHAMPIONS

U.S. Lawn Tennis:
    Men's Singles – Ken Rosewall
    Women's Singles – Shirley Fry

Wimbledon:
    Men – Lew Hoad (vs. Ken Rosewall)
    Women – Shirley Fry (vs. Angela Buxton)

Feel fresh again fast!

(RICHardson's cool, rich, zippy flavor does it)

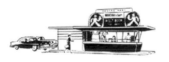

Now--enjoy 'em at home

Your favorite soda fountain milk shakes, sundaes, sodas in five take-home flavors!

Chocolate • Butterscotch • Strawberry • Pineapple • Walnut

RICHardson Corporation
Rochester 3, N. Y.

According to a New York City psychoanalyst, bullfighting is a Freudian unconscious acting out of the Oedipean battle between father and son for sexual supremacy. So, if you thought the sport was about pageantry, skill, danger and a lot of gore, get yourself to the nearest analyst's couch!

BOXING....

• KO •

● Rocky Marciano Retires Undefeated Heavyweight Champion Of The World After Winning All 46 Of His Pro Fights, 43 Of Which Were Knockouts.

● Floyd Patterson (21) Knocks Out Archie Moore In Title Fight, Becoming Youngest Boxer To Win Heavyweight Crown.

● Johnny Saxton Beats Carmen Basilio And Regains The World Welterweight Title.

CHESS

John Hudson, AAF Navigator, Wins U.S. Chess Federation Amateur Title Tournament.

WHAT A YEAR IT WAS!

AUTO RACING

Britain's Stirling Moss Wins Grand Prix Of Monaco Driving A Maserati.

PARACHUTING

French Fashion Model, Colette Duval, Breaks Her Own Women's World Record In Free-Fall Parachute Jump, Dropping 34,000 Ft. From A Plane Over Rio de Janeiro Before Opening Her Chute.

ROWING

Cornell Wins The Eastern Association Of Rowing Colleges Sprint Race.

BADMINTON

U.S. OPEN CHAMPIONSHIP

Men's Singles: Finn Kobbero, Denmark

Women's Singles: Judy Devlin, USA

VOLLEYBALL

Embarcadero (San Francisco) Wins U.S. Masters Title.
U.C.L.A. Wins Collegiate Title

PASSINGS

GRACE REIDY COMISKEY, president of Chicago White Sox (*1st woman president in American League*), dies at 62.

Clarence "Ginger" Beaumont, major league outfielder, first man to bat in a World Series game (1903), dies at 79.

1956 WAS A GREAT YEAR, BUT...

THE BEST IS YET TO COME!

PHOTOGRAPHY CREDITS

All photographs are courtesy of **FlikBaks**™ unless they are listed below. The author gratefully acknowledges the following contributions: